the Girl Who Ate everything

Easy Family Recipes from a Girl Who Has Tried Them All

Front Table Books • An Imprint of Cedar Fort, Inc. • Springville, UT

ISBN: 978-1-4621-1404-7

Published by Front Table Books, an imprint of Cedar Fort, Inc.
2373 W. 700 S., Springville, UT, 84663
Distributed by Cedar Fort, Inc., www.cedarfort.com

LIBRARY OF CONGRESS CATALOGING-IN-PUBLICATION DATA

Denney, Christy, 1980-
The girl who ate everything : easy family recipes from a girl who has tried them all / Christy Denney.
    pages cm
Includes index.
ISBN 978-1-4621-1404-7 (acid-free paper)
1. Quick and easy cooking. I. Title.
TX833.5.D456 2014
641.5'12—dc23
                    2014010821

Cover and page design by Erica Dixon and Bekah Claussen
Cover design © 2014 by Lyle Mortimer
Edited by Rachel J. Munk

Printed in the United States of America

10 9 8 7 6 5 4 3 2 1

To the greatest taste testers in the world:

My husband, John, and my kids, Austin, Brock, Weston, Grace, and Bailey.

Contents

Introduction

When I was newly married, I remember looking over at my six-foot-six, 260-pound husband and thinking, "How am I going to feed this man?" I hadn't cooked much up to that point, and I realized that I needed to learn quickly—really quickly. I started buying recipe books and trying out the recipes on my friends and family. There were many learning curves and a lot of epic fails, but I discovered along the way how much I relish cooking, especially because of the way it brings people together. I always knew I enjoyed eating food, but I learned then that I loved cooking just as much.

In 2008, my sister Sandra passed away unexpectedly at the age of 35. I was heartbroken. Most of my family lives in Arizona, and I struggled to cope with this trial on my own in Florida. I was in my kitchen one day, making a cherry cheese pie—a family favorite—and my pain eased a little as I remembered my sisters and I eating an entire cherry pie with no plates—just forks. We even promised to keep the pie a secret from our brothers, because we knew they wouldn't appreciate it like we did. For some reason, making family recipes proved to be my own kind of therapy; not to mention that it was a whole lot cheaper than buying premade food.

A few months later I started my blog, *The Girl Who Ate Everything*. I started by posting tried-and-true recipes from my family and friends. It was important to me to not only share stellar recipes, but also to tell the stories that went along with them. Every recipe has a story, and some are more intriguing than others. Whether it's how your grandma made her famous chocolate chip cookies, or how you covered yourself in flour the first time using your stand mixer, *EVERY* recipe has a story. At first, only my family read my blog, but slowly my readers grew in number. I am still in awe that so many people want to hear what I have to say, and actually make my recipes.

In 2010, General Mills asked me to write and develop recipes for them, and I agreed. I grew a lot working for them, and although I'm not a trained chef, there are certain tips and tricks that I learned along the way. Over time I learned skills like the basics of a roux and what flavors complement each other. I also discovered that I have a love for food photography and spent a lot of time researching and improving my knowledge in the area.

Over time, I developed a relationship with my readers; as much as I shared about my life, they shared back. I've met many people that I now consider great friends. Some I've met in person and some I have yet to meet. I get a lot of emails from readers saying that they never thought they could cook, but because of my blog, they've become passionate about cooking and have been successful at making delicious food. Those stories always make my day!

So many people ask me how I have time to cook, blog, and raise a family. My answer is: we all find time for things we love. Above all, my family comes first. My kids are always helping me in the kitchen and have actually become quite the little chefs. And although it does take some planning, I believe in sitting down every night for dinner as a family.

I've always tried to make our home a safe haven—warm and inviting, filled with people who love and care about each other. Half the neighborhood lives at our house—probably due to the overwhelming amount of baked goods available at all times. At dinner I like to go around the table and have everyone share their favorite part of the day. It keeps things positive and gives us a chance to talk about what's going on in each others' lives. Family dinners don't have to be complicated. I'm all about easy dinners, but if I have a recipe that takes a little more time, I will tell you up front. You can bet that it will be worth your time.

⮞⮞⮞ Tips and Tricks ⮜⮜⮜

Always use real butter.

Real butter makes all the difference, and I personally can tell in a recipe if something else was used. I always use unsalted butter in cooking—especially baking—so I can control the amount of salt in a recipe.

Parchment paper, parchment paper, parchment paper.

I use parchment paper for almost all of my baked goods. Cookies bake so much more evenly on it, and it prevents any kind of sticking.

Garlic.

I love garlic in everything. I don't always have fresh garlic cloves on hand, but the next best thing is a jar of minced garlic—it makes things so much easier.

Use fresh lemon and lime juice.

This is one situation where there are no shortcuts.
Fresh lemon and lime juice is so much better.

Eggs.

All my recipes that call for eggs refer to large eggs. It's remarkable how using extra-large eggs instead of large eggs can immensely alter the outcome of a recipe.

Keep a well-stocked kitchen.

I always have chicken breasts, beef, chicken broth, canned beans, and diced tomatoes on hand for quick and easy dinners.

appetizers

Antipasto Cups

My father-in-law has a salami sandwich almost every day for lunch, so I immediately thought of him when I came up with these. The salami gets crisp when baking, and is the perfect edible container to hold individual portions of this antipasto.

Ingredients

16 thin slices salami deli meat

1 (6-oz.) jar marinated artichoke hearts, drained and coarsely chopped

1 (6-oz.) jar roasted red peppers, drained and chopped

1 (4-oz.) can olives, drained

4 oz. fresh mozzarella cheese, cubed

2 Tbsp. fresh basil, sliced into ribbons

Instructions

Preheat oven to 400 degrees.

Place a slice of salami in the cup of each muffin tin. Bake for 8–10 minutes or until the salami is slightly crisp. Remove from the oven and let it cool. The salami might fold slightly when baking, but can be reformed once it is cool.

To assemble the cups: Place about a tablespoon each of the artichoke hearts, red peppers, olives, and mozzarella in each cup. Top with a ribbon of basil.

Makes 16 servings

Slow Cooker Creamy Bean Dip

There's something so good about a warm bean dip. It's an inexpensive appetizer that's also a crowd pleaser. I always crave this when I'm pregnant, and although that ship has sailed, it's still one of my favorites.

Ingredients

4 (16-oz.) cans refried beans

1 (8-oz.) pkg. cream cheese, softened

1 lb. Monterey Jack cheese, shredded

1 (.25-oz.) pkg. taco seasoning mix

1 cup chopped green onions

1 cup sour cream

Instructions

In a slow cooker, add all of the ingredients and stir to combine. Cook on low heat for 2–3 hours, stirring occasionally. Serve with chips.

Makes 16 servings

Mushroom Tarts

My neighbor, Julie, brought these over for me to try one day, and I couldn't figure out what the crust was made of. Who knew that regular sandwich bread could make the most wonderful crust? These tarts are a perfect two-bite appetizer, made of crusty sandwich bread with a buttery mushroom filling.

Ingredients

24 slices soft sandwich bread

4 Tbsp. butter

3 Tbsp. finely chopped shallots

1 cup sliced mushrooms

2 Tbsp. flour

1 cup heavy cream

½ tsp. crushed red pepper

1 Tbsp. chopped parsley

½ tsp. lemon juice

⅛ tsp. salt

2 Tbsp. grated Parmesan cheese

These can be made up to two days ahead of time and frozen. Prepare according to the directions below but reserve the Parmesan cheese in the last step until ready to bake. To bake, thaw tarts, sprinkle with reserved Parmesan cheese, and bake as instructed.

Instructions

Preheat the oven to 350 degrees and butter a mini muffin tin.

Cut each slice of bread into a circle using a 3-inch round biscuit cutter. You can also use the top of a drinking glass to cut your bread. Press circles into the mini muffin tin, gently forming into a cup. Bake for 5–6 minutes or until slightly toasted. Remove from the oven.

In a saucepan, melt the butter over medium heat. Add the shallots and cook until soft. Add the mushrooms and cook until they are tender and the juice has evaporated.

Sprinkle the mushrooms with flour and pour in the cream. Cook until thick. Add the red pepper, chopped parsley, lemon juice, and salt.

Fill the bread cups with the mushroom mixture. Sprinkle with Parmesan cheese and bake for 8–10 minutes or until the tarts are golden brown. Garnish with chopped parsley.

Makes 24 servings

Baked Sun-Dried Tomato Brie

One of life's greatest pleasures is ooey, gooey melted cheese. I was inspired by the flavors in a caprese salad when I came up with this appetizer. The sun-dried tomatoes, garden-fresh basil, and a touch of balsamic vinegar are the perfect complements to the buttery, flaky layers of the puff pastry.

Ingredients

1 sheet frozen puff pastry

1 (8-oz.) wheel Brie cheese, skin removed

¼ cup sun-dried tomatoes, chopped

1 Tbsp. chopped basil

1½ tsp. balsamic vinegar

1 egg white

1 Tbsp. water

Instructions

Preheat oven to 375 degrees.

Defrost the sheet of puff pastry for 15–20 minutes at room temperature and unfold.

Place the Brie in the center of the puff pastry and top with the tomatoes and basil. Drizzle with the balsamic vinegar.

Gather the edges of the puff pastry together around the Brie and press to seal. Beat the egg white and water together and brush over the pastry.

Bake for 20–25 minutes or until the puff pastry is golden brown. Let the Brie rest for 10 minutes before serving. Serve with crackers.

Makes 8 servings

Christy Denney

Individual Seven Layer Dips

I love seven layer dip. But after a few people have dug in, it starts to look messy and unappetizing. The problem is solved with these individually portioned dips. No double dipping!

Ingredients

1 (16-oz.) can refried beans

1 (1-oz.) pkg. taco seasoning

1 (8-oz.) container sour cream

1 cup guacamole

1 cup chunky salsa or pico de gallo

1 cup shredded Cheddar or Mexican blend cheese

2 Roma tomatoes, seeded and diced

1 (2.25-oz.) can sliced olives, drained

½ bunch of green onions, sliced

8 (9-oz.) plastic tumblers

tortilla chips

Instructions

In a small bowl, mix the taco seasoning with the refried beans.

In each plastic tumbler, layer about 2 tablespoons of the beans, followed by 2 tablespoons of sour cream, 2 tablespoons of guacamole, 2 tablespoons of salsa or pico de gallo, and 2 tablespoons of cheese. (Make sure you drain your salsa or pico to get the excess liquid out before you pour it on.) Then top each with about 1–2 teaspoons of tomatoes, olives, and green onion (if making ahead of time, wait to add these toppings until shortly before serving).

Garnish with one tortilla chip. Store in the refrigerator until serving and serve with chips.

Makes 8 servings

 I've found that when assembling the dips it helps to put some of the toppings, like the sour cream, in a large, resealable plastic bag and snip off the corner with scissors. Then you can easily pipe your topping into each cup quickly and without a mess.

Roast Beef Sliders

I know the combination may sound strange, but the mixture of walnuts, roast beef, and peach preserves will be a party in your mouth. Don't knock it 'til you try it. I love the creamy taste of Havarti, but feel free to use whatever cheese you prefer.

Ingredients

½ cup walnuts, finely chopped

2 Tbsp. mayonnaise

2 Tbsp. mustard

12 dinner rolls

¼ cup peach preserves

½ lb. thinly sliced deli roast beef, chopped

½ lb. thinly sliced Havarti cheese

Instructions

Preheat oven to 350 degrees.

In a small skillet, toast the walnuts for 4–5 minutes over medium heat. Set aside.

Combine the mayonnaise and mustard in a small bowl. Cut the dinner rolls in half and spread the mayonnaise/mustard mixture on each bottom roll.

On each top roll, spread about a teaspoon of peach preserves and sprinkle with walnuts. Place the roast beef and cheese on each bottom roll and close.

Place the sandwiches in a baking pan and cover with aluminum foil.

Bake for 20–25 minutes or until the cheese has melted. Serve immediately.

Makes 12 rolls

Restaurant Style Salsa

In under a minute, you can make ridiculously fresh-tasting salsa with ingredients you probably already have on hand. I like my salsa on the mild side, but if you want to up the heat factor, feel free to add another jalapeño.

Ingredients

½ cup coarsely chopped onion

½ cup cilantro

1 jalapeño, stem removed

1 clove garlic, minced

2 Tbsp. lime juice

½ tsp. salt

1 (28-oz.) can diced tomatoes, drained

Instructions

In a food processor add the onion, cilantro, jalapeño, and garlic and process until fine. Add the lime juice, salt, and tomatoes. Pulse gently until the salsa reaches the desired consistency. Add salt and pepper to taste.

Chill in the refrigerator for at least an hour to let the flavors blend together. Serve with tortilla chips.

Makes 10 servings

Cheeseburger Pizza Balls

I'm naturally drawn to any kind of game time food. I think most people would categorize us as a major sports family—and for good reason, since the majority of our life revolves around sports. I imagined these cheeseburger pizza balls in my mind, a blend of two foods I adore, and they were just as good as I hoped they would be. Not to mention they are the quintessential finger food to watch a game with.

Ingredients

¼ lb. ground beef

¼ cup diced onions

¼ cup ketchup

¼ cup mayonnaise

1 tsp. mustard

2 tsp. sweet relish

1 (7.5-oz.) pkg. 10-count refrigerated biscuits

1 cup shredded cheddar cheese

1 Tbsp. butter, melted

sesame seeds

optional toppings: lettuce, tomato, pickle

Instructions

Preheat the oven to 425 degrees and lightly spray a baking sheet with cooking spray.

In a skillet, brown the beef and onions over medium heat until the beef is no longer pink. Drain. Remove from heat and season with salt and pepper.

In a small bowl, combine the ketchup, mayonnaise, mustard, and sweet relish. Add half of the sauce to the beef and onion mixture, stirring to combine. Reserve the other half for dipping.

With the palm of your hand, flatten one biscuit at a time and lay it on the baking sheet. Add a heaping tablespoon of cheese and a tablespoon of meat on top of the biscuit. Gather the edges at the top, pinching them together to make a ball. Place the ball seam-side down on the baking sheet. Repeat with the remaining biscuits.

Brush each biscuit with melted butter and sprinkle with sesame seeds. Bake for 9–11 minutes or until the tops are golden brown.

Serve warm. Garnish with lettuce, tomato, and pickle if desired. Use the reserved sauce for dipping.

Makes 10 servings

Baked Coconut Shrimp with Spicy Orange Marmalade

I have an unwritten rule that I won't deep-fry foods—which is ironic because I don't blink an eye at using a pound of butter in a recipe. This baked coconut shrimp is a healthier version of the classic. The secret is to partially toast the coconut before coating the shrimp with it so that the shrimp and the coconut are done cooking at the same time.

Ingredients

2 cups sweetened coconut

1 lb. large shrimp, peeled and deveined

⅓ cup cornstarch

1 tsp. salt

2 egg whites, slightly beaten

Sauce

½ cup orange marmalade

1 tsp. Dijon mustard

1 tsp. prepared horseradish

Instructions

Preheat the oven to 400 degrees. Spray a baking sheet with cooking spray.

In a large skillet, add the coconut and cook for 5–6 minutes or until it is just starting to brown. Do not toast the coconut completely; it will continue to cook in the oven. Then place it in a shallow bowl.

Rinse the shrimp and pat them dry with paper towels. In a shallow bowl mix the cornstarch and salt. For each shrimp: Dredge the shrimp in the cornstarch mixture, dip in the egg whites, and then roll it in the toasted coconut. Place the shrimp on the baking sheet.

Bake the shrimp for 14–16 minutes or until no longer opaque, flipping halfway through the baking time.

For the sauce: Combine the orange marmalade, Dijon mustard, and horseradish in a small bowl. Serve with the shrimp for dipping.

Makes 4 servings

Creamy Corn Dip

Something about this corn dip is so addicting. It's best when it has chilled for a while to let all of the flavors blend together. I like to whip this one up when we have impromptu company over, because I always have the ingredients on hand.

Ingredients

2 (15.25-oz.) cans Fiesta corn niblets

2 (4-oz.) cans diced green chilies, drained

1 (4-oz.) can diced jalapeños, drained

½ cup chopped green onions

¾ cup mayonnaise

1 cup sour cream

1 tsp. ground pepper

1 clove garlic, minced finely

3 cups shredded cheddar cheese

Instructions

In a large bowl mix all the ingredients together. Refrigerate for at least 2 hours before serving. Serve with tortilla chips.

Makes 10 servings

Pizza Stuffed Mushrooms

They say your taste buds change every 7 years. I'm proof that that theory is actually true. I used to despise mushrooms, but after I got married I gave them another try, and have loved them ever since. Mushrooms are a blank canvas to which you can add any flavor that you love. I made the mistake of asking my kids what flavor of stuffed mushrooms we should make, and of course they said, "Pizza!"

Ingredients

½ lb. Italian sausage, casings removed

¾ cup chopped pepperoni slices, divided

⅓ cup finely chopped onion

1 (8-oz.) pkg. cream cheese, softened

½ cup pizza sauce

½ tsp. oregano

24 large white button mushrooms, wiped clean and stems removed

1 cup shredded mozzarella cheese

Instructions

Preheat the oven to 350 degrees and line a baking sheet with foil.

In a large skillet, cook the sausage, ½ cup of the chopped pepperoni, and the onion over medium heat for 5–6 minutes or until the sausage is brown. Drain. Reduce heat to low.

Add the cream cheese, pizza sauce, and oregano to the skillet. Stir and cook until melted. Remove from the heat.

Spoon a heaping tablespoon of the mixture into each mushroom cap and place on the baking sheet. Top the mushrooms with the remaining chopped pepperoni and sprinkle with the mozzarella cheese.

Bake for 18–20 minutes or until cheese is golden brown. Serve immediately.

Makes 24 servings

Peanut Butter "Cheese" Ball

This sweet "cheese" ball is by far one of the most popular recipes on my blog. Peanut butter and chocolate are my kryptonite. I may or may not have eaten an entire one of these by myself. In my defense, I was training for a marathon at the time. Peanut butter is packed with protein, right? Totally healthy.

Ingredients

1 (8-oz.) pkg. cream cheese, room temperature

1 cup powdered sugar

¾ cup creamy peanut butter

3 Tbsp. brown sugar

¾ cup peanut butter chips

¾ cup milk chocolate chips

graham cracker sticks or apple slices

 This can easily be made ahead of time and frozen until needed. Thaw at room temperature for 20–30 minutes before serving.

Instructions

Beat the cream cheese, powdered sugar, peanut butter, and brown sugar in large mixing bowl until blended.

Spoon the mixture onto a large piece of plastic wrap; bring up all four corners and twist tightly, forming into a ball shape.

Freeze for 1 hour 30 minutes, or until firm enough to keep its shape. Place the peanut butter and chocolate chips in a flat dish. Remove the plastic wrap from the ball and roll the ball into the morsels to completely cover, pressing the morsels into the ball if necessary.

Place the ball on a serving dish; cover and freeze for 2 hours or until almost firm. Serve with graham cracker sticks or apple slices for dipping or spreading.

Makes 10 servings

Baked Sriracha Chicken Drumsticks

My husband flies through bottles of Sriracha sauce, putting it on everything from fish to rice. He mixed it with barbecue sauce one evening at dinner, and ever since then we've been brushing the magical mixture on anything in sight.

Ingredients

3 lbs. chicken drumsticks

⅓ cup barbecue sauce

1½ Tbsp. Sriracha sauce

Instructions

Preheat the oven to 400 degrees.

Season the drumsticks with salt and pepper. Bake on a baking sheet for 30–40 minutes or until no longer pink, flipping halfway through.

In a small bowl, combine the barbecue sauce and the Sriracha sauce. Brush the mixture over the warm drumsticks.

Makes 10 servings

Creamy Artichoke Dip

Somewhere along the way I was nicknamed the "Dip Queen." Maybe I love dips so much because they get people talking and interacting around the kitchen table. This dip is on the spicy side, which makes my husband incredibly happy.

Ingredients

1 (14-oz.) can artichokes hearts, drained

1 (4-oz.) can diced green chilies, drained

1 cup mayonnaise

1 cup sour cream

1 jalapeño, seeded and minced finely

1 garlic clove, minced

3 cups shredded Mexican-blend cheese

½ cup grated Parmesan cheese

Instructions

Preheat the oven to 350 degrees.

Combine all of the ingredients in a food processor and process until combined. Pour into a shallow baking dish.

Bake for 20–25 minutes or until bubbly.

Serve with torn pieces of bread, chips, or vegetables.

Makes 12 servings

Ham and Cheese Roll Ups

These roll ups are a fun way to switch up the regular ham and cheese sandwich. I know it's not rocket science, but with just a few added ingredients, boring old ham and cheese sandwiches can become spectacular.

Ingredients

2 Tbsp. mayonnaise

2 Tbsp. Dijon mustard

16 slices soft sandwich bread

16 thin slices deli ham

16 thin slices Swiss cheese

2 Tbsp. butter, melted

Instructions

Preheat the oven to 350 degrees.

In a small bowl, combine the mayonnaise and mustard.

Cut the crusts off the bread and spread each piece with the mayonnaise/mustard mixture.

Lay a slice of ham on the bread and top with a slice of cheese. Roll up each piece of bread and place seam side down on a baking sheet.

Brush with melted butter and bake for 10–12 minutes or until golden brown.

Makes 16 servings

Buffalo Chicken Dip

My husband is obsessed with anything "buffalo" flavored. My sister-in-law, Kimi, created this dip years ago, and on any given game day you can bet we'll be eating it in our house. I've probably made this dip over 100 times.

Ingredients

1½ cups cooked and shredded chicken

½ cup Frank's RedHot Buffalo Wings Sauce

1 (8-oz.) pkg. cream cheese, softened

½ cup ranch dressing

¾ cup shredded cheddar cheese

blue cheese crumbles (optional)

Instructions

Preheat the oven to 350 degrees. Stir the chicken and Buffalo sauce in a skillet over medium heat until heated through.

Stir in the cream cheese and the ranch dressing. Cook, stirring until well blended and warm. Mix in the shredded cheese.

Pour the mixture into a shallow dish or pie pan and sprinkle with the blue cheese crumbles, if desired. Bake for 10–15 minutes or until hot and bubbly. Serve with chips, carrots, and celery for dipping.

Makes 8 servings

If you can't get enough of the blue cheese flavor, replace the ranch dressing with blue cheese dressing.

Tomato Pesto Tart

They say you can grow anything in Florida. I, however, am the exception to that rule, because everything I try to grow dies. I can only imagine how delicious this tart would be with tomatoes fresh from the garden. For now, I'll have to settle for store-bought tomatoes, but believe me when I say that this tart is still out of this world.

Ingredients

1 (13.8-oz) container refrigerated pizza crust

2 cups shredded mozzarella cheese, divided

2 tomatoes, thinly sliced

¼ cup Parmesan cheese

½ cup mayonnaise

½ tsp. minced garlic

2 Tbsp. basil pesto

½ tsp. ground pepper

Instructions

Preheat the oven to 425 degrees and lightly spray a 14 × 12 rectangular baking sheet. Press the pizza dough evenly into the baking sheet and prick it with a fork. Bake for 6–8 minutes or until lightly browned.

Sprinkle the dough with 1½ cups of the mozzarella cheese and top it with the tomato slices.

In a small bowl, combine the Parmesan cheese, mayonnaise, garlic, remaining ½ cup of mozzarella, pesto, and pepper. Spread the mixture over the tomatoes.

Bake for an additional 10–12 minutes or until golden brown. Cut into slices and serve.

Makes 10 servings

breads and rolls

One-Hour Rolls

I don't always have patience for all the work that rolls entail, and usually only make them for special occasions. These one hour rolls, however, are so simple that you can let them rise while you're making dinner and enjoy warm buttery bread with your meal. Just because they're quick doesn't mean you're sacrificing anything. What I love most about these rolls is their fluffy texture.

Ingredients

1 cup warm water

¼ cup sugar

⅓ cup oil

2 (.25-oz.) pkg. yeast

1 tsp. salt

1 egg, beaten

3⅔ cups flour

1 Tbsp. butter, melted

 I've lost the thermostat war at my house. My husband keeps our house at arctic cold temperatures so sometimes it's difficult to get my dough to rise. Over the years, I've learned a secret to creating a warm place for my dough to rise. I heat my oven to 200 degrees, turn the oven off, and place my dough inside. It works perfectly every time.

Instructions

In a large bowl, mix together the warm water, sugar, oil, and yeast. Let it stand for 15 minutes until the yeast mixture is bubbly.

Stir the salt and beaten egg into yeast mixture.

Gradually mix in the flour. Add flour until the dough is no longer sticky. Cover the dough and let it rise for 10 minutes in a warm place.

Spray your hands with non-stick cooking spray and form the dough into balls. Place the balls on a cookie sheet and let them rise for 20 more minutes.

Bake in a 375 degree oven for 10–12 minutes. Brush with melted butter while warm.

Makes 18 servings

Bubble Bread

We often go on our vacations to the west coast of Florida, where there's a certain restaurant known for its bread. I tried my best to recreate the famous bread on my own. The secret ingredient to this magical bread is a tiny touch of blue cheese in the cheese mixture, which is spread on top and baked. Blue cheese haters won't even know it's there. It just gives the bread that little extra tang that makes this bread so unique.

Ingredients

¼ cup butter, softened

1 Tbsp. crumbled blue cheese

2 Tbsp. mayonnaise

½ cup shredded Swiss cheese

¾ cup grated Parmesan cheese, divided

1 (12-oz.) Italian or French bread loaf, sliced lengthwise

¼ tsp. dried parsley

Instructions

In a small bowl, mix the butter, blue cheese, mayonnaise, Swiss cheese, and ½ cup of the Parmesan together in a bowl. Spread the mixture on top of both slices of bread.

Sprinkle the remaining ¼ cup Parmesan cheese on top of each slice and sprinkle it with parsley.

Broil at 500 degrees for 6 minutes, or until brown and bubbly.

Makes 12 servings

Bloomin' Cheddar Bacon Ranch Bread

This bread earned its name from its flower-like shape. I've found that you can stuff it with whatever toppings you like, but I really love this version with cheddar cheese, bacon, and ranch drizzled on top. This bread is a conversation starter! I've made it with other round artisan breads but have found that I love the slightly tart taste, and the sturdy texture of sourdough makes the cutting process easier.

Ingredients

1 round, unsliced loaf sourdough bread

8-12 oz. cheddar cheese, thinly sliced

1 cup cooked, crumbled bacon

6 Tbsp. butter, melted

1 rounded Tbsp. unprepared ranch dressing mix

½ tsp. garlic powder

2 Tbsp. sliced green onions

Instructions

Preheat the oven to 350 degrees.

Using a serrated knife, cut the bread lengthwise and width-wise without cutting through the bottom crust. It can be a little tricky slicing the second direction, but the bread is usually very forgiving.

Place on a foil-lined baking sheet. Insert the cheese slices between the cuts. Sprinkle crumbled bacon in between the slits and on the top.

Combine the melted butter, dry ranch dressing mix, and garlic powder in a small bowl. Drizzle it over the bread. Top it with green onions.

Wrap the bread in foil completely and place it on a baking sheet. Bake for 15 minutes.

Unwrap the bread and bake for an additional 5–10 minutes, or until the cheese is melted and the top is golden brown.

Tear pieces off and eat. Dip in prepared ranch dressing if desired.

Makes 8 servings

Outrageous Banana Bread

My sister-in-law, Laura, has a really good banana bread recipe, and I decided to take it even more over the top by adding a cream cheese filling and a crumbly streusel topping. This may have a few more steps than the average recipe, but the result is quite a masterpiece.

Ingredients

Bread
¾ cup butter, softened

2 eggs

1½ cups brown sugar

3 cups mashed ripe bananas

1½ tsp. baking soda

½ tsp. salt

1 tsp. vanilla

½ tsp. cinnamon

2½ cups flour

Filling
1 (8-oz.) pkg. cream cheese, softened

⅓ cup sugar

1 egg

Streusel Topping
⅓ cup sugar

⅓ cup flour

1½ tsp. cinnamon

2 Tbsp. butter, softened

Instructions

Preheat the oven to 325 degrees and spray two medium foil loaf pans with cooking spray.

Cream the butter, eggs, brown sugar, and bananas with a mixer. Add the baking soda, salt, vanilla, cinnamon, and flour. Mix well.

Divide half of the batter equally between the two loaf pans.

For the filling: In a small bowl, combine the cream cheese, sugar, and egg. Divide the cream cheese mixture in half and spread it over the bread batter. Spread the remaining batter on top of the cream cheese mixture in both pans.

For the streusel: Combine all of the ingredients and mix well until crumbly. Sprinkle over the top of the bread batter.

Bake for 55–60 minutes. Cover with foil if the top is beginning to brown too much.

Makes 8 servings

Bridian's Pizza Dough and Breadsticks

Bridian is the first person besides family that I ever let babysit my kids. She's been making dinner for her own family of eight ever since she was little. She usually quadruples this dough when making it, and it still disappears within minutes.

Ingredients

Pizza dough
1¼ cups very warm water

1 (.25-oz.) pkg. yeast

1 Tbsp. sugar

1 tsp. salt

3 cups flour

Breadsticks
2 Tbsp. butter, melted

garlic salt

onion powder

dried parsley

dried oregano

grated Parmesan cheese

½ cup finely shredded cheddar cheese

1 cup marinara sauce for dipping

Instructions

In a large bowl, add the warm water and the yeast. Let the yeast dissolve. Add the sugar, salt, and 2 cups of the flour. Mix well.

Add another ½ to 1 cup flour. Keep adding it a little at a time until the dough is no longer sticky. Knead it by hand or mix with a stand mixer for 1–2 minutes. On an oiled counter, roll the dough out to ½-inch thickness. If making pizza, let it rise until doubled.

If making breadsticks, brush the melted butter all over the crust. Sprinkle garlic salt, onion powder, parsley, oregano, grated Parmesan cheese, and cheddar cheese on top. These measurements are all approximate.

Cut the dough into strips and let them rise to 1-inch thickness for 45–60 minutes.

Bake the pizza or breadsticks at 500 degrees for 6 minutes. Dip in warm marinara sauce.

Makes 16 servings

Orange Rolls

Like I've said before, I really didn't start cooking until I got married. I dabbled a little in college, and my roommate Lisa showed me that cooking can be easy and fun. For my wedding present, Lisa and my other roommate, Jill, gave me a recipe box filled with handwritten recipes they loved, including this one. These rolls melt in your mouth and have a bright citrus flavor. Thanks, ladies, for the gift that keeps on giving.

Ingredients

Rolls
2 cups milk

½ cup sugar

½ cup oil

3 tsp. salt

6 cups flour

2 eggs

2 (.25-oz.) pkg. yeast

½ cup warm water

Filling
½ cup butter, softened

1 cup sugar

grated peel of 1 orange

Glaze
juice of 1 orange

2½ cups powdered sugar

Instructions

In a large bowl stir the milk, sugar, oil, and salt together until the sugar is completely dissolved. Add 2 cups of the flour and beat well. Add the eggs and stir them in.

Dissolve the yeast in the warm water and add it to the flour mixture. Mix in the remaining 4 cups of flour. At this point, you can knead the dough with a stand mixer, or knead it by hand for 5 minutes. Put the dough into a greased bowl and let it rise until double (about an hour) in a warm place.

Divide the dough into 6 parts and roll each into a circle.

Mix the filling ingredients together. Cover each circle with one-sixth of the filling mixture and cut it into 8 wedges like a pizza.

Roll each into a crescent shape. Cover and let them rise at least 1 hour in a warm place.

Bake at 400 degrees for 8–10 minutes. Do not overbake! It's normal for a little of the filling to leak out.

While the rolls are baking, prepare the glaze.

For the glaze: The measurements are approximate. I like to juice the orange and then add powdered sugar until I reach my desired consistency. Brush the glaze onto the warm rolls.

Makes 4 dozen rolls

Sheri's Pumpkin Bread

I make myself wait until October 1st every year to begin baking with pumpkin. I'm an all-or-nothing girl, and I've found that in order to not burn myself on pumpkin treats, I had to make this rule. The first thing I make is my mother-in-law's famous pumpkin bread. Some pumpkin breads have a hint of spice, but this bread is chock full of spices and is incredibly moist.

Ingredients

4 egg yolks

1 cup oil

⅔ cup water

1 (15-oz.) can pumpkin pie puree

3 cups sugar

1½ tsp. salt

1 tsp. cinnamon

1 tsp. nutmeg

2 tsp. baking soda

3½ cups flour

Instructions

Preheat oven to 350 degrees. Spray three medium loaf pans with cooking spray.

Mix together the egg yolks, oil, water, and pumpkin puree. Add the sugar, salt, cinnamon, nutmeg, baking soda, and flour and mix well.

Pour the batter evenly into the loaf pans. Bake for 50–60 minutes. Don't overcook. Wrap them in plastic wrap while warm.

Makes 3 loaves

Let the bread cool slightly, but wrap it in plastic wrap while it is still warm. This traps all the moisture inside and keeps your bread unbelievably moist. I love this bread even better the second day, when all the flavors have blended together. Make sure you use pumpkin pie puree, not pumpkin pie filling.

breakfast

Mini Puff-Puff Pancakes

Puff-puff pancakes, or German pancakes, are some of my favorite pancakes to make on Saturday mornings because I always have the ingredients on hand. These mini versions are individually portioned. They earn their name by puffing up in the oven, and then naturally falling, creating a little well to fill with fruit or your desired topping.

Ingredients

6 eggs

1 cup flour

1 cup milk

½ tsp. salt

1 tsp. vanilla extract

¼ cup butter, melted

Instructions

Preheat the oven to 400 degrees and spray two muffin tins well with cooking spray.

In a large bowl mix all of the ingredients together well. Fill each muffin tin halfway with the batter.

Bake for 15–17 minutes or until the pancakes are golden on the edges.

Remove from the tins and serve with fruit, maple syrup, and powdered sugar.

Makes 18 pancakes

Eggs Benedict Casserole

I love Eggs Benedict, but the whole process can be a little fussy and time-consuming for me. Instead of tediously making individual portions, it's a whole lot easier for me to layer the ingredients in a casserole pan. I have a hard time not licking the Hollandaise sauce off my plate when I make this.

Ingredients

¾ lb. Canadian bacon, diced

6 English muffins, split and cut into 1-inch pieces

8 eggs

2 cups milk

1 tsp. onion powder

⅓ cup chopped green onions

Hollandaise Sauce

4 egg yolks

¼ tsp. Dijon mustard

1 Tbsp. lemon juice

½ cup butter, melted

Instructions

Spray a 9 × 13 baking dish with cooking spray.

Spread half of the Canadian bacon in the bottom of the dish. Cover it with the diced English muffins. Top with the remaining Canadian bacon.

In a medium bowl, combine the eggs, milk, onion powder, and green onions. Beat them until combined. Pour the mixture over the casserole. Cover and refrigerate for at least 8 hours.

After the casserole has chilled, preheat the oven to 375 degrees. Bake for 30–35 minutes or until the center is set.

For the Hollandaise Sauce: In a double boiler, add the eggs, mustard, and lemon juice. Cook over medium heat, stirring constantly. Reduce the heat to low and slowly drizzle in the butter while whisking. Make sure not to overheat the sauce.

Drizzle the Hollandaise Sauce immediately over the casserole and serve.

Makes 12 servings

Slow Cooker Banana Walnut Oatmeal

Making oatmeal in the slow cooker is a great idea in theory, but with regular oats, the end result can be a mushy mess. The only way to cook oatmeal in a slow cooker is to use steel-cut oats, which can withstand the long cooking process and hold their shape. The kitchen will smell like banana bread all morning when you make this comforting oatmeal.

Ingredients

2 Tbsp. unsalted butter

2 cups steel-cut oats

7½ cups water

4 ripe bananas, mashed

1 cup walnuts, toasted

¾ cup brown sugar

1 tsp. salt

½ tsp. cinnamon

Instructions

In a skillet, melt the butter over medium heat. Add the oats and cook for 2–3 minutes, until fragrant.

Spoon the oats into a 4-quart slow cooker. Add the water, bananas, walnuts, brown sugar, salt, and cinnamon. Stir to combine.

Cook in the slow cooker for 4–6 hours on low. Let cool slightly before serving.

Makes 8 servings

Jelly Roll Pancakes

This recipe comes from my mother-in-law, Sheri. She's been making these for years, and my husband used to make them every Friday for his seminary students. They have a unique texture. They're thicker than crepes, but thinner than pancakes. It's hard for me to eat less than 10 of these at a time, and I've even eaten them cold out of the refrigerator. My husband likes them with butter and jam. My favorite way to eat them is with butter and a sprinkle of sugar.

Ingredients

4 eggs, beaten

3 cups milk

1 tsp. vanilla extract

3 cups flour

½ cup sugar

½ tsp. salt

butter for pan

Toppings

powdered sugar

granulated sugar

syrup

jam

Nutella

Instructions

In a large bowl, add all the ingredients and mix until well combined.

Melt some butter in a skillet over medium-low heat and cook the batter as you would regular pancakes, 2–3 minutes per side. The key is to cook on low heat until the pancakes are no longer glossy and they are barely golden.

Spread each pancake with your desired toppings. Roll them up and eat!

Makes 6 servings

Broccoli Cheese Pie

I've been making this pie for my family for years now. It's great for brunch, but I admit that most of the time I make it for dinner, just to switch things up. This pie has broccoli and mushrooms on top of a cheesy crust.

Ingredients

4 cups broccoli florets, chopped

Crust

1½ cups shredded cheddar cheese

1 cup flour

½ tsp. salt

¼ tsp. dry mustard

6 Tbsp. butter, melted

Filling

1 Tbsp. butter

1 onion, chopped

1 cup sliced mushrooms

2 Tbsp. flour

1 cup half-and-half

½ tsp. salt

¼ tsp. ground nutmeg

3 eggs, beaten

Instructions

Preheat the oven to 400 degrees.

Steam the broccoli until tender.

For the crust: In a small bowl, mix the cheddar cheese, flour, salt, and mustard. Mix in the butter until well combined. Press the mixture into the bottom and sides of a 9-inch pie dish.

For the filling: Melt the butter in a skillet over medium heat and sauté the onion and mushrooms until soft. Stir in the flour, half-and-half, salt, and nutmeg. Bring the mixture to a boil and cook for 1 minute or until the mixture thickens.

Remove the filling from the heat. Mix in the steamed broccoli and slowly stir in the eggs. Pour the mixture into the pie crust.

Bake for 15 minutes in the preheated oven. Reduce the heat to 350 degrees and bake an additional 15 minutes, or until a knife inserted in the center comes out clean.

Makes 8 servings

Christy Denney

Egg Sonora

Here's another recipe that comes from my old roommate, Lisa. It's a no-fuss, one-bowl breakfast casserole that feeds a crowd. I'm not usually a big cottage cheese fan, but it completely disappears when baking in this dish.

Ingredients

10 eggs

½ cup flour

1 tsp. baking powder

½ tsp. salt

½ cup butter, melted

2 cups cottage cheese

4 cups shredded mozzarella cheese

1 cup chopped green chilies

Instructions

Preheat the oven to 350 degrees and grease a 9 × 13 baking dish.

In a large bowl, beat the eggs well. Add the flour, baking powder, and salt and mix until combined. Add all the remaining ingredients; mix well.

Pour the mixture into the prepared pan and bake for 30–45 minutes or until the center is set. Cover with foil after 30 minutes if the top is getting too brown.

Cool slightly and cut into squares. Serve with a dollop of sour cream and diced tomatoes, if desired.

Makes 12 servings

Blueberry Breakfast Crumble

This breakfast dish is made from buttery biscuits, rolled in brown sugar and layered with oats and blueberries. I have to restrain myself from eating the whole thing. While most of the time fresh is the only way to go, blueberries freeze well and can absolutely be used frozen in this dish.

Ingredients

½ cup light brown sugar

1 tsp. cinnamon

1 (12-oz.) can buttermilk biscuits

½ cup butter, melted

1 cup quick-cooking rolled oats

1½ cups fresh or frozen blueberries

¼ cup sugar

Instructions

Preheat the oven to 350 degrees and grease a 9-inch square baking dish.

In a small bowl, combine the brown sugar and cinnamon and mix well. Cut each biscuit into quarters. Dip each piece in melted butter and roll in the cinnamon mixture. Arrange the pieces in a single layer in the baking dish. Sprinkle with half of the oats.

In another small bowl, combine the blueberries and sugar and toss to coat. Spoon over the oats and biscuits and sprinkle with remaining ½ cup oats. Bake for 20 minutes or until the top is golden brown and the center is done. Cool slightly and serve warm.

Makes 6 servings

Crème Brûlée French Toast

Have I mentioned that I'm not a morning person? I thought that having kids would turn me into a morning person, but now I just have little ones to witness as I struggle to perk up in the morning. So basically the less I have to do in the morning the better, which is why I love this Crème Brûlée French Toast, which is prepared the night before. The sauce caramelizes on the bottom while baking, creating a thick layer of sweetness. I always feel that overnight French toast can have Goldilock's syndrome. It can often be too dry or too wet, but this one is just right.

Ingredients

½ cup unsalted butter

¾ cup brown sugar

1 Tbsp. corn syrup

8–10 1-in. thick slices French bread

4 eggs

1 cup half-and-half

2 tsp. vanilla extract

¼ cup orange juice

¼ tsp. salt

orange zest for garnish

Instructions

In a small saucepan, melt the butter over medium heat. Add the brown sugar and corn syrup and cook until sugar has dissolved. Pour into a 9 × 13 baking dish. Arrange slices of the French bread in a single layer on top of the sugar mixture.

In a medium bowl, add the eggs, half-and-half, vanilla, orange juice, and salt. Whisk until combined. Pour the mixture over bread slices. Cover tightly and refrigerate for at least 8 hours.

Preheat the oven to 350 degrees and take the baking dish out of the refrigerator to come to room temperature as your oven heats up.

Bake uncovered for 30–40 minutes. Remove from the oven and immediately flip the dish upside-down onto a serving plate. Garnish with orange zest and serve.

Makes 8 servings

This recipe calls for French bread, but you can also use a loaf of challah or brioche. Any of these breads are suitable for soaking up all of the liquid overnight.

Snickerdoodle Muffins

Snickerdoodles for breakfast? They might not be cookies, but these muffins have the same taste after being dipped in butter and rolled in a cinnamon sugar mixture. These are best when served warm. If you can't eat them fresh out of the oven, pop them in the microwave for 10 seconds to get them nice and warm.

Ingredients

6 Tbsp. butter, softened

½ cup sugar

1 egg

½ cup milk

1 tsp. vanilla extract

1½ cups flour

1½ tsp. baking powder

¾ tsp. cream of tartar

¼ tsp. salt

½ tsp. cinnamon

Topping

⅓ cup sugar

1 tsp. cinnamon

2 Tbsp. butter, melted

 Make sure your baking powder has not expired. Since most of us don't use it very often, there's a tendency to forget that it expires, and your rising power is depleted.

Instructions

Preheat the oven to 350 degrees and grease a mini muffin tin.

In a medium bowl, beat the butter and sugar until fluffy. Add the egg, milk, and vanilla and mix to combine.

In a separate bowl, whisk together the flour, baking powder, cream of tartar, salt, and cinnamon.

Add the flour mixture to the egg mixture slowly. As soon as the flour mixture is combined, stop stirring! Overmixing your batter can result in hard muffins.

Fill each muffin tin ¾ of the way full. Bake for 9–11 minutes. For regular size muffins, bake for 14–16 minutes.

In a small bowl, combine the sugar and cinnamon. Remove the muffins from the tin. Dip the tops of the muffins in the melted butter and roll them in the cinnamon sugar mixture. These are best served warm.

Makes 2 dozen

Eggs in a Cloud

We eat a LOT of eggs in my family. Boiled, scrambled, poached. . . you name it, we'll eat it. The whites of these eggs are whipped until soft and mixed with cheese, onions, and bacon. You can add whatever toppings float your boat into the egg whites. Then each yolk is gently placed in a cloud of egg whites, and the whole thing is baked for just a few minutes. They look intimidating, but they are totally doable and are equally impressive.

Ingredients

4 eggs

¼ cup shredded cheddar cheese

¼ cup chopped green onions

¼ cup cooked and crumbled bacon

Instructions

Preheat the oven to 450 degrees and line a baking sheet with parchment paper.

Put the yolks in 4 separate small bowls. Whip the egg whites until stiff peaks form. Fold in the cheese, onions, and bacon. Spoon the egg whites onto a prepared baking sheet and make an indentation in each of them.

Bake for 3 minutes. Remove from the oven and gently add a yolk to each well. Bake for 2–3 minutes or until yolk is set. Serve immediately.

Makes 4 servings

Strawberry Coconut Croissant Bread Pudding

If you've never had bread pudding made with croissants, you are missing out. The flaky, buttery layers in this dish are just begging to be soaked in a creamy coconut milk mixture and baked. I love any dish with a tropical taste, and this had me feeling like I was having breakfast in Hawaii.

Ingredients

5 cups croissants, torn into 2-inch pieces

½ cup coconut, toasted

½ cup diced strawberries

4 eggs

½ cup sugar

1 cup coconut milk

1 cup heavy cream

1½ tsp. vanilla extract

Instructions

Lightly grease a 9-inch square baking dish.

Place the croissants, coconut, and diced strawberries in the prepared pan and toss to combine.

In a separate bowl add the eggs and beat slightly. Add the sugar, coconut milk, cream, and vanilla and whisk until combined. Pour the mixture over the croissants. Cover and refrigerate for at least 4 hours.

After the mixture has chilled, remove it from the refrigerator and preheat the oven to 350 degrees.

Bake uncovered for 40–50 minutes, covering with foil if the tops of the croissants start to get too brown.

Serve warm or at room temperature.

Makes 6 servings

main dishes

Pasta Milano

Mushrooms, sun-dried tomatoes, and basil are mouthwatering additions to this pasta and cream sauce. This is a dish I like to make for company because it always gets fantastic reviews and looks like a fancy shmancy entrée that you would order at a restaurant.

Ingredients

12 oz. bow tie pasta

2 Tbsp. oil

1 lb. boneless skinless chicken breast halves

2 cups sliced mushrooms

2 cloves garlic, minced

½ cup sun-dried tomatoes packed in oil, drained and chopped

1 cup chicken broth

2 cups heavy cream

1 tsp. Dijon mustard

2 Tbsp. chopped fresh basil

Instructions

Cook the pasta in salted water until firm, or al dente, according to the package directions.

While the pasta is cooking, heat the oil in a large saucepan over medium heat. Add the chicken and cook for 3–4 minutes per side or until done. Remove and keep the chicken warm on a plate. Slice into bite-sized pieces.

Add the mushrooms, garlic, and sun-dried tomatoes to the saucepan and cook until the mushrooms are tender.

Add the chicken broth, cream, Dijon mustard, and basil to the mushroom mixture. Bring the mixture to a boil, stirring constantly. Reduce it to medium heat and continue to cook until the sauce thickens to desired consistency, about 10 minutes.

In a large bowl, toss the chicken, pasta, and cream sauce together. Add salt and pepper to taste. Serve immediately.

Makes 6 servings

Island Pork Tenderloin

My nephew's wife, Aimee, graduated in culinary arts and could certainly teach anyone a little something in the kitchen. She gave me this recipe for a unique pork tenderloin. The cinnamon in the spice rub scared me a little at first, but it all blends together to give this dish its island flair.

Ingredients

2 lbs. pork tenderloin

1 Tbsp. oil

Rub

1 tsp. salt

½ tsp. pepper

1 tsp. chili powder

1 tsp. ground cumin

1 tsp. cinnamon

Glaze

½ cup brown sugar

1 Tbsp. finely minced garlic cloves

1 Tbsp. hot sauce

Instructions

Preheat the oven to 350 degrees and combine the ingredients for the spice rub in a small bowl.

Coat the tenderloin with the spice rub.

In a large skillet, heat the oil on high heat and brown the pork on all sides, sealing in the flavor and moisture.

Place the pork in a roasting pan. Stir together the glaze and spoon it on top of the tenderloin.

Bake for 20–30 minutes, or until the pork reaches a desired doneness.

Makes 10 servings

Homestyle Chili

This chili was inspired by a hearty chili that I discovered at a local fast food joint. I tweaked and tested it until I felt like it tasted similar to the original, and I think it's pretty spot on. Regardless, it's a chunky chili full of flavor. I love throwing this in the slow cooker while we're at a football game and coming home to a warm, comforting dinner.

Ingredients

2 lbs. ground beef

1 cup chopped onion

1 (29-oz.) can tomato sauce

1 (29-oz.) can kidney beans, with liquid

1 (29-oz.) can pinto beans, with liquid

1 (15-oz.) can diced tomatoes, drained

1 (4-oz.) can diced green chilies

¼ cup diced celery

2 tsp. ground cumin

3 Tbsp. chili powder

1½ tsp. black pepper

2 tsp. salt

1 cup water

toppings: sour cream, cheese, green onions

Instructions

In a large skillet, brown the beef and onion. Drain.

Add the beef mixture to a slow cooker, along with all the remaining ingredients, and cook on low for 4–6 hours.

Serve with the sour cream, cheese, and green onions.

Makes 12 servings

Chicken Pesto Stuffed Shells

Whenever I make these stuffed shells I make 2 pans, one for dinner that night and one for later. It's also a great take-in meal to friends who are sick or have just had a baby.

Ingredients

24 jumbo pasta shells

2 cups cooked, shredded chicken

4-oz. cream cheese, softened

¼ cup basil pesto

⅔ cup ricotta cheese

½ teaspoon salt

½ cup grated Parmesan cheese

½ tsp. onion powder

2 cloves garlic, minced

2 cups marinara sauce

 These stuffed shells can be made ahead of time and frozen until needed. Just thaw and cook as instructed in the recipe.

Instructions

Preheat the oven to 350 degrees and spray a 9 × 13 baking dish with cooking spray.

Prepare the pasta shells according to the package directions.

In a medium bowl, stir together the chicken, cream cheese, pesto, ricotta, salt, Parmesan, onion powder, and garlic.

Spoon the mixture into the cooked pasta shells and place them in the baking dish.

Top each shell with a large spoonful of marinara sauce.

Cover the dish with aluminum foil and bake, covered, for 20–25 minutes. Sprinkle with additional Parmesan cheese and serve.

Makes 24 shells

Christy Denney

Nacho Beef Casserole

This casserole was inspired by my favorite childhood meal that my mom used to make. Think gourmet nachos in casserole form.

Ingredients

2 lbs. ground beef

1 onion, chopped finely

1 (16-oz.) pkg. frozen corn kernels

2 (16-oz.) cans chili beans

1 (15-oz.) can tomato sauce

1 (.25-oz.) pkg. taco seasoning

3 cups shredded cheddar cheese, divided

3 cups slightly crushed nacho cheese tortilla chips

toppings: sour cream, diced tomatoes, and green onions

 To dress up this casserole, spoon some sour cream into a resealable plastic bag, cut off the corner, and pipe a drizzle across the whole casserole.

Instructions

Lightly grease a 9 × 13 baking dish.

In a Dutch oven, cook and stir the beef and onion over medium heat for 5–8 minutes or until the beef is no longer pink. Drain.

Add the corn, chili beans, tomato sauce, and taco seasoning and stir until combined. Cook over medium heat for about 5 minutes or until all of the ingredients are warmed through.

Spoon half of the meat mixture into the baking dish and top with 1½ cups crushed chips and 1½ cups cheese.

Pour the remaining half of the meat mixture on top and add the remaining 1½ cups crushed chips and 1½ cups cheese.

Bake for 20–25 minutes or until hot and bubbly.

Drizzle with sour cream and top with diced tomatoes and green onions.

Makes 10 servings

Juicy Beef

If I could eat beef tenderloin every night, I most certainly would. However, since tenderloins are on the expensive side, you can replace it with another cut of beef. This juicy sauce makes any cut of beef tender. Even though it's only made from two ingredients, people always ask what is in this sauce. They're blown away when they find out how simple it is.

Ingredients

1 (3-lb.) beef tenderloin roast

⅓ cup unsalted butter, melted

½ cup low-sodium soy sauce

Instructions

Preheat the oven to 350 degrees. Place the beef in a baking dish and pour the melted butter and soy sauce on top. Bake for 45 minutes or until the meat has reached your desired doneness. Let the meat rest for 10 minutes to allow the juices to redistribute before cutting.

Makes 10 servings

Chicken Caesar Pasta Casserole

It's a pasta dish that tastes like a chicken Caesar salad! You can use any pasta you like, but I like the shape of the rotini because it really soaks in the Caesar dressing. My kids love croutons as much as they love pasta so this dish really makes them happy.

Ingredients

2 cups rotini pasta, uncooked

2 cups cooked and shredded chicken

1 cup creamy Caesar dressing

½ cup chicken broth

⅓ cup diced green onions

1½ cups garlic flavored croutons, crushed

¼ cup Parmesan cheese

Instructions

Preheat the oven to 350 degrees and grease a 2-quart baking dish.

Prepare the pasta according to the package directions.

In a large bowl, combine the chicken, Caesar dressing, chicken broth, green onions, and cooked pasta.

Pour the mixture into the prepared baking dish and top it with the crushed croutons. Sprinkle Parmesan cheese on top and bake, uncovered, for 20–25 minutes or until the croutons are golden brown. Serve with a green salad.

Makes 6 servings

Hawaiian Grilled Chicken with Coconut Rice

Back in college, my friend Jeff was famous for his Hawaiian grilled chicken. He was nice enough to pass on the recipe to me. You're going to be tempted to use chicken breasts, but trust me—chicken thighs hold the moisture and flavor so much better. The chicken has a very subtle coconut flavor that is complemented by the coconut rice.

Ingredients

3 lbs. boneless skinless chicken thighs

1 cup low-sodium soy sauce

1 cup water

1 cup brown sugar

1 bunch green onions, chopped (reserve half for garnish)

½ tsp. minced garlic

1 tsp. sesame oil

1 (13.5-oz.) can coconut milk

 Coconut rice can be made by replacing half of the water with coconut milk when preparing your rice.

Instructions

Trim the chicken thighs of any visible fat.

In a large bowl, mix the soy sauce, water, brown sugar, half of the green onions, garlic, sesame oil, and coconut milk in a large bowl. Marinate the chicken in the refrigerator for at least 8 hours, or overnight, to make sure the flavor is infused.

Grill the chicken at a low heat so the marinade does not burn, for 5–7 minutes per side, or until done. If you do not have a grill you can use a indoor grill pan.

Serve over a platter of coconut rice and garnish chicken with the remaining green onions and some additional soy sauce.

Makes 8 servings

Brazilian Rubbed Salmon

In South Florida we live in a melting pot of different cultures. One of my friends from Brazil gave me this salmon recipe. I love the citrus flavor mixed with the sweet and spicy glaze.

Ingredients

4 (6-oz.) salmon fillets

2 Tbsp. fresh orange juice

1 Tbsp. fresh lemon juice

salt and pepper

1 tsp. orange zest

2 Tbsp. brown sugar

1 Tbsp. chili powder

1 garlic clove, minced

2 Tbsp. butter, melted

Instructions

Marinate the salmon in the orange juice, lemon juice, salt, and pepper for 20 minutes at room temperature. Discard any remaining marinade. Preheat the oven to 425 degrees.

In a small bowl, combine the orange zest, brown sugar, chili powder, and garlic. Rub well onto the marinated salmon.

Grease a foil-lined baking sheet with cooking spray. Place the salmon on the sheet and drizzle butter on top.

Bake for 14–18 minutes, depending on the thickness of the fillets. Garnish with lemon and orange wedges.

Makes 4 servings

Buffalo Chicken Pizza

My husband started drooling when I pulled this out of the oven. Ranch dressing is used as the sauce for this pizza, and it's topped with buffalo chicken pieces and a sprinkle of blue cheese. If you're an avid blue cheese lover, use blue cheese dressing instead of the ranch for the pizza sauce.

Ingredients

1 pizza dough ball (or use Bridian's Pizza Dough on p. 46)

½ cup ranch dressing

1½ cups cooked, shredded chicken

½ cup Buffalo wing sauce

2 cups shredded mozzarella cheese

2 Tbsp. blue cheese crumbles

Instructions

Preheat the oven to 500 degrees. Press the pizza dough onto a pizza pan. Prick it with a fork several times and bake for 5–6 minutes.

Remove the crust from oven and spread ranch dressing all over pizza. In a small bowl, combine the chicken and the Buffalo sauce. Distribute the chicken evenly over the pizza. Cover the pizza with the mozzarella and sprinkle with blue cheese crumbles. Bake for 4–5 minutes or until the cheese starts to brown.

Makes 8 servings

Creamy Asparagus Chicken

Growing up, my mom made a chicken asparagus casserole that I could never get enough of. This is an updated twist on that casserole, minus the canned soup and made with individual chicken breasts for a prettier presentation.

Ingredients

¼ cup mayonnaise

1½ Tbsp. Dijon mustard

1 Tbsp. lemon juice

¼ tsp. salt

1 tsp. ground pepper

16 spears asparagus, trimmed

4 boneless skinless chicken breast halves, pounded thin

4 slices provolone cheese

1 cup Panko bread crumbs

2 Tbsp. butter, melted

Instructions

Preheat the oven to 350 degrees and grease a 9 × 13 baking dish.

In a small bowl, mix together the mayonnaise, Dijon mustard, lemon juice, salt, and pepper. Set aside.

Cook the asparagus in the microwave on high for 1–2 minutes until tender.

Brush each chicken breast with the mayonnaise mixture and place 3–4 asparagus spears on top. Top each chicken breast with one slice of provolone cheese.

Mix the Panko bread crumbs with butter and sprinkle on top of the cheese.

Bake for 25–30 minutes or until the chicken juices run clear.

Makes 4 servings

Italian Beef Sandwiches

The meat in these sandwiches falls apart in your mouth, it's so tender. The secret to its intense flavor is to add a little bit of juice from the pepperoncinis to the meat while cooking.

Ingredients

3 lbs. boneless beef chuck pot roast

1 (15-oz.) can tomato sauce with Italian seasonings

1 green bell pepper, sliced

1 onion, sliced

1 (12-oz.) jar pepperoncini salad peppers, drained and stems removed (reserve ½ cup juice)

1 (.7-oz.) dry Italian dressing mix

12 sandwich rolls, split and toasted

Instructions

Place the meat in a 6-quart slow cooker. Pour the tomato sauce over the meat. Top with the pepper, onion, pepperoncini peppers, and the reserved juice. Sprinkle with the dry Italian dressing.

Cover and cook on low for 10–12 hours, or on high for 5–6 hours. Transfer the meat to a cutting board. Shred it with two forks and return it to the slow cooker.

Use a slotted spoon to spoon the meat mixture onto the rolls. Use the sauce for dipping.

Makes 8 servings

Chicken Pot Pie Crumble

What's the best part about a pie? The crust, of course! This chicken pot pie has an overload of crust crumbles on top with a savory, vegetable-packed filling inside. This recipe may take a little extra time to make, but it is totally worth it.

Ingredients

Crumble

1¼ cups flour

1½ tsp. baking powder

½ tsp. salt

¼ tsp. freshly ground black pepper

4 Tbsp. butter, cold and cut into small cubes

½ cup grated Parmesan cheese

¾ cup heavy cream

Filling

1 lb. skinless, boneless chicken breast halves, cubed

1 (16-oz.) bag frozen carrots and peas

½ cup sliced celery

1 (32-oz.) carton chicken broth (reserve 1¾ cups for sauce)

⅓ cup chopped onion

⅓ cup butter

⅓ cup flour

½ tsp. salt

¼ tsp. black pepper

¼ tsp. celery seed

⅔ cup milk

Instructions

Preheat the oven to 425 degrees and grease a deep-dish pie pan.

For the crumble: In a medium bowl, whisk together the flour, baking powder, salt, and pepper. Using your hands, cut the butter into the mixture until it resembles wet sand. Stir in the Parmesan cheese. Add the cream and mix until just combined. Drop 2-inch pieces of dough onto a parchment lined baking sheet. Bake for 8–10 minutes. Remove from the oven and set aside.

For the filling: In a large pot, combine the raw chicken, carrots, peas, and celery. Add the carton of chicken broth to cover, and boil everything for 15 minutes. Remove it from the heat, drain (reserving 1¾ cups chicken broth for filling), and set aside.

In the saucepan over medium heat, cook the onions in the butter until soft and translucent. Stir in the flour, salt, pepper, and celery seed. Slowly stir in the reserved chicken broth and milk. Simmer over medium-low heat until it becomes thick. Remove it from the heat and combine it with the chicken, carrots, peas, and celery mixture. You can add more chicken broth if you like, depending how runny you want your filling.

Place the filling in pie pan. Top with the crumble pieces. Place a cookie sheet underneath the pie pan to catch any spills.

Bake for 8–10 minutes, or until the top is golden brown and the filling is bubbly. Cool for 10 minutes before serving.

Makes 8 servings

Burrito Casserole

If it's Mexican you're craving, this burrito casserole will satisfy your palate. This is absolutely one of the simplest, most satisfying meals you will ever make.

Ingredients

1 lb. ground beef

½ cup chopped onion

1 (1¼-oz.) pkg. taco seasoning

1 (10-oz.) can diced tomatoes with green chilies

1 (16-oz.) can refried beans

1 (10.75-oz.) can cream of mushroom soup

½ cup sour cream

6 large flour tortillas

3 cups shredded Mexican-blend cheese

½ cup salsa

Instructions

Preheat the oven to 350 degrees and grease a 2-quart casserole dish.

In a large skillet over medium heat, brown the beef and onion. Drain.

Add the taco seasoning, diced tomatoes, salsa, and refried beans and stir to combine.

Mix the cream of mushroom soup and sour cream in a separate bowl. Spread half of the mixture on the bottom of the casserole dish.

Tear half of the tortillas into pieces and spread over the sour cream mixture.

Spread half of the meat mixture on top of the tortillas. Sprinkle half of the cheese on top of the meat.

Repeat with the remaining sour cream mixture, tortillas, meat mixture, and cheese.

Bake for 20–30 minutes or until hot.

Top with additional sour cream, tomatoes, and green onions if desired.

Makes 12 servings

Parmesan Dijon Crusted Chicken Tenders

I like to think of these as dressed-up chicken nuggets for adults. It's hard to make meals that make both adults and kids happy, but this is definitely one of them. These tenders are coated in a spiced-up Dijon mustard and rolled in a crunchy coating. Although these aren't fried, baking them at a high temperature gets the outside extra crispy.

Ingredients

2 Tbsp. Dijon mustard

½ tsp. salt

¼ tsp. pepper

¼ tsp. chili powder

¾ cup crushed cornflakes

¾ cup grated Parmesan cheese

4 chicken breasts, cut into strips

Instructions

Preheat the oven to 450 degrees and place a wire rack over a foil lined pan. Spray the rack lightly with cooking spray.

Mix together the mustard and spices in a small bowl. In a shallow bowl, mix the cornflakes and Parmesan.

Brush the chicken with the mustard mixture and then roll in the cornflake mixture. Place on the rack.

Bake for 15–20 minutes or until done.

Makes 4 servings

Creamy Sausage and Tomato Pasta

This recipe comes from a reader of the blog whose husband, it turns out, played football with my husband in college. The recipe quickly became a family favorite, and the aroma in the kitchen of basil, garlic, and tomatoes when cooking this meal is unbelievable. It always has the kids running in saying, "What's that yummy smell, Mom?" Thanks, Wylie, for the great recipe.

Ingredients

12 ounces penne pasta

4-5 (about 1 lb.) spicy Italian sausages

1 cup chopped onion

3 cloves garlic, minced

1 (16-oz.) can Italian style diced tomatoes

1 (8-oz.) can tomato sauce

1 cup heavy cream

5-6 big leaves of fresh basil, chopped

grated Parmesan for topping

Instructions

Cook the pasta in salted water until firm, or al dente, according to the package directions.

While the pasta is cooking, remove the casings from the sausage and brown the meat for 5–6 minutes or until done. Drain the fat.

Add the onions and garlic to the sausage and sauté for 1–2 minutes.

Pour the diced tomatoes and tomato sauce into the sausage mixture and heat through.

Pour in the cream and stir for 1–2 minutes. The longer you cook the sauce, the thicker it will get, so simmer it until it is the consistency you want.

Add the fresh basil and let it simmer for a few minutes.

When the pasta is done, drain and mix it with the sausage sauce in a large bowl; serve. Top each serving with a sprinkle of Parmesan cheese. Serve with garlic bread.

Makes 6 servings

Sweet and Sour Meatballs

I'm really picky about my sweet and sour meatballs. It's hard to find the right balance between the two flavors, but this sauce is just right. Usually I try to use lean ground beef when I'm cooking with beef, but for meatballs you actually want to use a less lean cut to keep them moist.

Ingredients

Meatballs
1½ lbs. 80/20 ground beef

¾ cup quick rolled oats

2 eggs

½ cup chopped onion

1 tsp. salt

1 tsp. Worcestershire sauce

Sauce
½ cup brown sugar

¼ cup vinegar

1 tsp. prepared mustard

¼ cup barbecue sauce

1 tsp. Worcestershire sauce

Instructions

Preheat oven to 350 degrees.

For the meatballs: In a large bowl, combine the beef, oats, eggs, onion, salt, and Worcestershire. Roll the mixture into 12 balls and place in a 9 × 13 baking dish.

In a small bowl combine all of the sauce ingredients. Pour the sauce over the meatballs.

Bake for 30 minutes or until cooked through.

Makes 12 servings

Aunt Janet's Chicken and Wild Rice Soup

I don't think I've ever eaten a dish from my Aunt Janet that wasn't to die for. She gave me this recipe for creamy chicken soup with wild rice. This soup has just the right consistency—not too thick and not too thin. It's such a comforting meal on a cold night.

Ingredients

4 chicken breasts, cooked and diced

3 celery stalks, chopped

3 carrots, sliced

1 onion, diced

Cream Sauce

4 Tbsp. butter

⅔ cup flour

3 cups chicken broth

3 cups vegetable broth (reserved from cooked vegetables)

1½ cup half-and-half

1½ cups cooked wild rice

Instructions

Bring a large pot of water to a boil. Add the celery, carrots, and onion and boil until tender. Drain, reserving 3 cups of water for the cream sauce.

For the cream sauce: In a saucepan, melt the butter over medium heat and add the flour. Cook and stir until thick.

Slowly add the chicken broth, reserved vegetable broth, and half-and-half. Continue simmering and stirring until soup thickens. Add the vegetables, cooked wild rice, and chicken and warm it all together. Add more rice if you want a thicker texture. Serve.

Makes 6 servings

Pizza Mac

Pizza and macaroni and cheese in one? Pretty much a kid's dream, right? I really love the flavors in pizza and mixed with pasta turns out to be one tasty dish. For those of you who don't love cottage cheese, you won't even notice it in this dish, I promise!

Ingredients

1 lb. elbow macaroni

1 (16-oz.) jar pizza sauce

2 cups cottage cheese

½ white onion, chopped finely

½ green bell pepper, chopped finely

1 clove garlic, minced

1 tsp. dried Italian seasoning

1 (6-oz.) pkg. sliced pepperoni

2 cups shredded mozzarella cheese, divided

¾ cup grated Parmesan cheese, divided

Instructions

Preheat the oven to 350 degrees and spray a 9 × 13 baking dish with cooking spray.

Cook the pasta according to the package directions, using heavily salted water.

In a large bowl, combine the cooked pasta, pizza sauce, cottage cheese, onion, bell pepper, garlic, and Italian seasoning. Take half of the pepperoni and cut it into quarters. Stir together the chopped pepperoni, 1 cup of the mozzarella cheese, and ½ cup of the Parmesan cheese.

Pour this mixture into the prepared pan and top it with the remaining pepperoni. Sprinkle with the remaining 1 cup of mozzarella and ¼ cup Parmesan cheese and bake uncovered for 20–25 minutes.

Makes 10 servings

Chicken and Dumpling Casserole

Have you ever done one of those recipe exchanges where you mail 6 recipes out and you are supposed to get 36 back? Usually you're lucky if you get any back, but I actually did, and that's where this recipe came from. This is comfort food at its bes—savory vegetables in a creamy sauce, topped with quick biscuits.

Ingredients

½ cup chopped onion

½ cup chopped celery

2 garlic cloves, minced

¼ cup butter

½ cup flour

2 tsp. sugar

1 tsp. salt

1 tsp. dried basil

½ tsp. pepper

4 cups chicken broth

1 (10-oz.) pkg. frozen peas

4 cups cubed, cooked chicken

Dumplings

2 cups Bisquick

1 tsp. dried basil

⅔ cup milk

Instructions

Preheat oven to 350 degrees and grease a 9 × 13 baking dish.

In a large saucepan, sauté the onion, celery, and garlic in butter until tender. Add the flour, sugar, salt, basil, pepper, and broth. Bring everything to a boil. Cook and stir for one minute. Reduce the heat. Add the peas and cook for 5 minutes, stirring constantly. Stir in the cooked chicken.

For the dumplings: Combine the Bisquick and basil. Stir in the milk with a fork until just moistened. Drop in about 12 spoonfuls onto the casserole. Bake for 30 minutes. Cover and bake for 10 minutes more or until done.

Makes 12 servings

Grilled Salmon with Lime Butter

We love to eat salmon in our house. My kids even refer to it as pink chicken, which is funny, because I don't ever want them really eating pink chicken. My friend Kendee gave me this recipe, and I fell in love with the lime butter sauce. I want to pour it on everything.

Ingredients

6 (6-oz.) salmon fillets

1½ tsp. finely grated fresh lime zest

½ cup butter, melted

1 garlic clove

¼ cup fresh lime juice

1 tsp. salt

½ tsp. pepper

Instructions

Heat the grill to medium-high heat and lightly oil grill grate

Season the salmon with salt and pepper. Grill 4–5 minutes per side or until fish flakes easily with a fork.

Remove salmon from the grill and sprinkle it with the lime zest.

In a blender, add the butter, garlic, lime juice, salt, and pepper. Blend until completely combined.

Drizzle the sauce over the grilled salmon.

Makes 6 servings

Slow Cooker Loaded Baked Potato Soup

There's nothing like coming home to a warm soup that's been cooking all day in the slow cooker. This soup has a flavorful base, just begging to be "loaded" with your favorite baked potato toppings.

Ingredients

2 Tbsp. butter

1 onion, minced

3 garlic cloves, minced

2 Tbsp. flour

4 cups chicken broth

6 medium potatoes, peeled and cut into ½-inch pieces

2 cups shredded cheddar cheese, extra for topping

½ cup heavy cream

½ cup cooked, crumbled bacon

3 green onions, sliced thin

sour cream

salt and pepper to taste

Instructions

In a saucepan, melt the butter over medium-high heat. Add the onion and garlic and cook until the onion is soft.

Stir in the flour and cook for one minute. Slowly stir in 1 cup of the chicken broth. Transfer the mixture to the slow cooker.

Add the potatoes and the remaining 3 cups of chicken broth to the slow cooker.

Cover and cook on low for 4–6 hours, or until potatoes are fork tender.

Take 2 cups of the cooked potatoes out of the slow cooker and place them in a medium bowl. Mash until smooth.

Stir the cheese into the soup until combined. Stir in the mashed potatoes and cream.

Serve the soup with bacon, green onions, sour cream, and cheese.

Makes 6 servings

Weeknight Turkey Burgers

We have these turkey burgers so often I could make them in my sleep. They're healthy and hearty. If you want to make them extra healthy, replace the bun with a large piece of lettuce. If you're not a turkey lover, there are a couple of tricks to make the turkey meat taste more like your classic beef burger, like adding steak seasoning and a couple of splashes of Worcestershire sauce. My mom taught me a secret—to add really finely chopped onion to the meat. It's undetectable and gives it great flavor.

Ingredients

1 (20-oz.) pkg. 70/30 ground turkey

¼ cup finely diced white onion

1 egg white

1 Tbsp. Worcestershire sauce

1 clove garlic, minced

1 Tbsp. bread crumbs

1 tsp. steak seasoning

hamburger buns

toppings: lettuce, tomato, onion, cheese, ketchup, mustard

Instructions

Preheat the grill to medium heat and oil well.

In a large bowl, combine the turkey, onion, egg white, Worcestershire, garlic, bread crumbs, and steak seasoning. Add salt and pepper as needed. Mix together and form into 5 patties.

Grill the burgers for 4–5 minutes per side or until done. Add a slice of cheese to the top of each burger a minute before removing from the grill, if desired. Place the burgers on buns and top with your favorite toppings.

Makes 5 servings

Mom's White Chicken Chili

My mom cooks for 30 people every Sunday, regardless of whether or not anyone comes over, so everyone seems to gravitate toward her house so a meal never goes to waste. She usually makes a ton of this chili, but I scaled it back a bit to make it the perfect size to serve my family.

Ingredients

6 (15-oz.) cans great northern beans, drained and rinsed

3 (4-oz.) cans diced green chilies

½ cup butter

1 onion, diced finely

½ cup flour

1 (32-oz.) can chicken broth

3 tsp. ground cumin

2–3 cups shredded rotisserie chicken

2 cups shredded Monterey Jack cheese

1 cup sour cream

dash of hot sauce (optional)

Instructions

In a 6-quart slow cooker, add the beans and chilies.

In a large pot or Dutch oven, melt the butter over medium heat. Add the onion and cook until soft. Sprinkle the flour in the pot and continue to cook for 1–2 minutes. Slowly add the chicken broth, stirring constantly. Pour the liquid into the slow cooker and stir to combine.

Add the cumin and chicken. Cook on low for 4–6 hours.

Before serving, stir in the cheese and sour cream. Add hot sauce if desired. Serve with tortilla chips.

Makes 10 servings

Robbie's Barbecue Brisket

My friend Heidi made her mother-in-law's brisket for us for Christmas dinner years ago; we've adopted the tradition and have made it for Christmas every year since then. My kids like to call it the "roast beast." Liquid smoke is the secret to making beef taste like it's been roasting away all day. All of the measurements are approximate, but I tried to nail down exactly how I make it every year.

Ingredients

5 lbs. beef brisket

2 Tbsp. Worcestershire sauce

4 Tbsp. liquid smoke

2 tsp. onion powder

1 tsp. garlic powder

salt and pepper

1 (20-oz.) bottle barbecue sauce

 You can make this beef ahead of time and store it in the refrigerator until serving. 30 minutes before serving, take barbecue sauce and reserved juice from the brisket and pour it over the sliced brisket. Bake uncovered for 30 minutes or until the meat is heated thoroughly and the sauce is bubbly.

Instructions

Preheat the oven to 325 degrees.

In a large baking pan, place a long strip of heavy duty foil lengthwise across the pan (long enough to be able to fold back on each end to encase the brisket). Place a second strip over the first, but in the opposite direction.

Place the brisket on the foil in the pan and season as follows: Pour Worcestershire and liquid smoke over the brisket and sprinkle with the onion powder, garlic powder, salt, and pepper.

Fold the first strip of foil up on both sides until ends meet. Roll the ends together to meet the brisket. Repeat on the other length of the foil. Seal the foil on all edges by folding it over and toward the top of the brisket.

Bake for 4–5 hours, or until tender when pierced with a fork.

Drain the juices from the corner of the pan, reserving ½ cup of the juice for the sauce.

Remove the brisket from the foil and carefully place it on a carving board.

Using a very sharp carving knife or electronic carving knife, cut the brisket into ¼-inch slices against the grain.

Transfer the slices back into the baking pan carefully.

In a small saucepan, combine the barbecue sauce and reserved juice from the pan and simmer until hot. Pour over the brisket slices and serve.

Makes 8 servings

Pesto Chicken Pasta

This is one of those weeknight meals that I like to have in my back pocket, for days when dinner time comes around and I have no game plan. Pesto is the secret weapon here, giving you fresh flavor without a lot of ingredients.

Ingredients

8 oz. penne pasta

2 Tbsp. butter

2 Tbsp. olive oil

2 cloves garlic, minced

4 boneless skinless chicken breasts, cut into 2-inch pieces

1¼ cups heavy cream

¼ cup basil pesto

¼ cup grated Parmesan cheese

salt and pepper to taste

Instructions

Prepare the pasta according to the package directions.

In a large skillet, heat the butter and olive oil over medium heat. Add the garlic and chicken, cooking for 4–5 minutes on each side or until the chicken is cooked through.

Reduce the heat and stir in the cream, pesto, and Parmesan. Add salt and pepper to taste. Stir in the cooked pasta and serve.

Makes 4 servings

Salsa Verde Chicken

I love using salsa verde in recipes because the tomatillos, onion, and spices are already bottled inside for an easy punch of flavor. You can use this chicken in tacos, burritos, or on top of a salad for a healthy dinner.

Ingredients

2 lbs. boneless skinless chicken breasts

½ tsp. minced garlic

¼ tsp. ground cumin

salt and pepper

1 (16-oz.) jar salsa verde

Instructions

Place the chicken in a 4-quart slow cooker and spoon the minced garlic over it. Sprinkle the chicken with the cumin, salt, and pepper and pour the salsa verde on top. Cook on low for 4–6 hours.

Remove the chicken from the slow cooker and shred. Put back in the slow cooker and stir in the juice. Serve with a slotted spoon and use the chicken on a salad or in tacos.

Makes 4 servings

Easy Baked Rigatoni

This pasta is a simple and easy weeknight dinner that my whole family loves. The Italian sausages pack a whole lot of spice into the dish.

Ingredients

12 oz. rigatoni pasta

3 spicy Italian sausages, casings removed

1 Tbsp. extra virgin olive oil

½ cup diced onion

½ green bell pepper, seeded and diced

2 garlic cloves, minced

salt and pepper to taste

2½ cups marinara sauce

1 cup shredded mozzarella cheese

½ cup grated Parmesan cheese

In pasta dishes, it's really important to heavily salt the water to season your noodles while they're cooking. Otherwise, you'll have bland pasta.

Instructions

Preheat the oven to 350 degrees and grease a 9-inch square baking dish.

Prepare the pasta according to the package directions. Drain and place back in the pot.

Add the sausage to a skillet over medium-high heat and cook until browned and crumbly. Drain and add to the pasta.

Discard the leftover grease and add the olive oil to the pan. Add the onion, bell peppers, and garlic to the pan and sauté for 3–4 minutes or until veggies are soft. Season with salt and pepper. Pour the onion mixture over the sausage and pasta mixture and toss together.

Add the marinara, ½ cup of the mozzarella, and ¼ cup of the Parmesan. Toss together until combined.

Pour mixture into the prepared dish and top with the remaining mozzarella and Parmesan.

Bake for 20–25 minutes or until the cheese starts to brown. Cool slightly and serve.

Makes 6 servings

salads and sides

Apple Broccoli Salad

I always pay attention to what disappears first at get-togethers, and this broccoli salad is one of the first things to go. I like adding apples to mine—for an extra crunch and for their fresh sweetness.

Ingredients

Salad

4 cups broccoli florets

2 cups diced apples

½ cup cooked and crumbled bacon

½ cup coarsely chopped pecans, toasted

½ cup raisins

½ red onion, chopped

Dressing

1 cup mayonnaise

½ cup sugar

2 Tbsp. apple cider vinegar

Instructions

In a medium bowl, add all of the salad ingredients and toss together.

In a small bowl, combine the mayonnaise, sugar, and vinegar and add to the broccoli mixture. Stir well.

Cover and store in the refrigerator. Chill the salad for at least an hour before serving.

Makes 6 servings

Avocado Chicken Salad

The classic chicken salad has tons of mayonnaise in it. This chicken salad is lightened up a bit, using mashed avocados in place of some of the mayonnaise, making it healthier without sacrificing the creamy texture.

Ingredients

1 cup pecan halves

1½ cups cooked and diced chicken

1 cup sliced celery

1½ cups grapes, halved

¼ cup mayonnaise

2 ripe avocados, peeled, pitted and mashed

1 tsp. lemon juice

salt and pepper

Instructions

In a small skillet, cook the pecans over medium heat for 5–6 minutes or until toasted. Set aside.

In a medium bowl, add all of the ingredients and mix well to combine. Season with salt and pepper.

Makes 6 servings

Chicken Apricot Feta Salad with Citrus Vinaigrette

This is a light and refreshing salad topped with apricots, feta, chicken, and almonds, and tossed with a tangy vinaigrette. I use apricots, but you can use any dried fruit and any nut that you like.

Ingredients

Citrus Vinaigrette

2 Tbsp. fresh squeezed orange juice

1 tsp. Dijon mustard

2 Tbsp. apple cider vinegar

2 Tbsp. honey

2 Tbsp. extra virgin olive oil

Salad

8 cups chopped green leaf or romaine lettuce

½ cup sliced and toasted almonds

½ cup feta

½ cup dried apricots, quartered

1½ cups cooked and cubed chicken

salt and pepper

Instructions

For the dressing: Add all of the ingredients to a small bowl and whisk well until combined.

In a large bowl, add the lettuce, almonds, feta, apricots, and chicken. Drizzle dressing over the salad and toss to combine.

Makes 6 servings

Whenever I'm making a salad for company, I set aside a small portion of the toppings for sprinkling on after I've tossed the salad. Add the reserved toppings on top of the salad for a beautiful presentation.

Spinach Salad with Poppy Seed Dressing

My sister-in-law Tracy has been making her amazing spinach salad for as long as I've known her. Her version feeds a small army, so I've downsized it so it's just enough to feed my family.

Ingredients

Salad

5 cups spinach

5 cups chopped romaine lettuce

½ cup cooked and crumbled bacon

1½ cups fresh sliced mushrooms

½ cup sliced red onion

2 cups shredded mozzarella cheese

Dressing

¼ cup red wine vinegar

½ cup oil

½ tsp. dry ground mustard

¼ cup sugar

1½ tsp. poppy seeds

½ tsp. salt

Instructions

For the salad: In a large bowl, toss together the spinach, lettuce, bacon, mushrooms, onion, and cheese.

For the dressing: In a small bowl, whisk together all of the dressing ingredients until combined. Toss the salad with the dressing right before serving to keep it from getting soggy.

Makes 6 servings

Chicken Fiesta Salad

I could eat Mexican food every day of my life. Maybe it's because I grew up in Arizona, or maybe I just love the flavors. This salad is made up of fresh vegetables, lettuce, and seasoned chicken breasts, and is drizzled with a chipotle ranch dressing. You might want to make a double batch of dressing and use it for, well, practically everything.

Ingredients

Dressing
1 chipotle pepper (in adobo sauce)
½ cup buttermilk
½ cup mayonnaise
2 tsp. lime juice
⅓ cup cilantro leaves
½ tsp. ground cumin
½ tsp. garlic powder
¼ tsp. dried oregano
½ tsp. salt

Chicken
1 tsp. chili powder
½ tsp. ground cumin
½ tsp. salt
¼ tsp. pepper
2 (6-oz.) boneless, skinless chicken breasts, sliced in half lengthwise
2 Tbsp. vegetable oil

Salad
10 cups chopped green leaf or romaine lettuce
1 (15-oz.) can black beans, rinsed and drained
1 (11-oz.) can corn, drained
½ red onion, sliced
1 large tomato, seeded and diced
1 avocado, diced
tortilla strips (optional)

Instructions

For the dressing: Add all of the ingredients to a blender and blend until smooth. Chill in the refrigerator until serving.

For the chicken: In a small bowl, combine the chili powder, cumin, salt, and pepper. Pat the chicken breasts dry with a paper towel and rub the mixture onto the chicken. Heat the oil in a 12-inch skillet. Add the chicken and cook until golden brown for 6–8 minutes. Remove the chicken from the skillet and keep covered on a plate.

For the salad: In a large bowl, combine the lettuce, black beans, corn, onion, tomato, and avocado. Toss lightly. Slice the cooked chicken and lay it on top of the greens. Drizzle with dressing and top with tortilla strips if desired.

Makes 4 servings

 No need to throw out the remaining chipotle peppers in the can. Most recipes only call for one or two peppers, and the rest can be placed in a small plastic resealable bag and frozen for later.

Greek Salad

One of my go-to healthy snacks is a small cup of fresh tomatoes, onions, cucumber, and feta with a dash of vinegar. By adding just a few more ingredients, I turned it into a fabulous Greek salad tossed with a light vinaigrette.

Ingredients

Salad

10 cups chopped romaine lettuce

2 tomatoes, cut into wedges

½ red onion, sliced

1 cup olives

1 small cucumber, seeded and diced

4 oz. crumbled feta cheese

Dressing

2 Tbsp. lemon juice

¾ cup olive oil

¼ cup red wine vinegar

1 tsp. dried oregano

½ tsp. dried basil

½ tsp. salt

½ tsp. pepper

2 cloves garlic, minced

¼ cup grated Parmesan cheese

Instructions

In a large bowl, combine the lettuce, tomatoes, red onion, olives, cucumber, and feta.

Blend all of the dressing ingredients in a blender until combined.

Toss the salad with the dressing and serve.

Makes 8 servings

Tortellini Salad

This salad has layers of greens, tomatoes, bacon, tortellini, and ranch dressing. The beauty of this salad is that you can customize it to your preferences and add whatever toppings you wish. If you're not a fan of ranch, use blue cheese or your favorite dressing.

Ingredients

1 cup milk

1 cup mayonnaise

1 (1-oz.) pkg. ranch dressing mix

9 oz. cheese tortellini

3 cups chopped romaine lettuce

3 cups spinach

2 cups grape or cherry tomatoes, halved

½ cup cooked, crumbled bacon

½ cup chopped green onions

Instructions

In a small bowl, combine the milk and mayonnaise with the ranch dressing mix. Cover and refrigerate for 30 minutes to thicken.

Prepare the tortellini according to the package directions. Cool.

In a large glass bowl, layer the salad in this order: lettuce, spinach, tortellini, tomatoes, prepared dressing, bacon, and green onion.

Refrigerate until ready to serve.

Makes 10 servings

Pear and Quinoa Salad

My friend Caryn gave me this recipe and I fell in love with it. It's a quinoa salad filled with pears, green onions, bacon, spinach, and almonds and tossed with an Asian-inspired dressing.

Ingredients

Salad

1 cup quinoa

2 Bartlett pears, peeled and diced

2 green onions, sliced

4 slices of bacon, cooked and crumbled

1-2 cups fresh spinach, coarsely chopped

1 red bell pepper, diced

¼ cup sliced almonds, toasted

Dressing

⅓ cup vegetable oil

⅓ cup rice vinegar

2 Tbsp. soy sauce

2 tsp. sesame oil

¼ tsp. minced garlic

2 Tbsp. sugar

¼ tsp. ground ginger

Instructions

Prepare the quinoa according to the package directions. 1 cup dry quinoa should yield over 4 cups of cooked quinoa. Cool quinoa.

In a large bowl, add the cooled quinoa, pears, green onions, bacon, spinach, bell pepper, and almonds.

For the dressing: Combine all of the dressing ingredients in a small bowl and pour over the quinoa mixture. Toss gently. You might not want to use all of the dressing, depending on how moist you want your salad, so add a little at a time. Add salt and pepper to taste.

Chill in the refrigerator for at least an hour before serving so the flavors can meld.

Makes 6 servings

Creamed Spinach

I'm all about shortcuts, but in this recipe fresh spinach makes all the difference. This recipe can easily be doubled for a larger crowd. This creamed spinach is a wonderful side to a steak like the Juicy Beef on page 91.

Ingredients

2 Tbsp. butter

1 Tbsp. olive oil

½ cup finely minced onion

1 garlic clove, minced

10 oz. spinach, coarsely chopped

2 Tbsp. cream cheese, softened

¼ cup heavy cream

¼ tsp. ground nutmeg

¼ cup shredded Parmesan cheese

Instructions

In a large saucepan, melt the butter and olive oil over medium heat.

Add the onion and garlic; cook for 1–2 minutes or until the onion is soft and translucent.

Add the spinach to the pan and cook for 3–4 minutes or until the spinach starts to wilt.

Stir in the cream cheese and heavy cream. Cook until the mixture thickens.

Add the nutmeg and Parmesan cheese and stir to combine. Add salt and pepper to taste. Serve immediately.

Makes 4 servings

Easy Garlic Mashed Potatoes

I detest peeling potatoes, so these garlic mashed potatoes are a dream to me. The potatoes are cooked and mashed with the skins on, and then seasoned to perfection.

Ingredients

8 small red potatoes, unpeeled and quartered

1 tsp. salt

¼ tsp. fresh ground black pepper

3 cloves garlic, minced

½ cup sour cream

½ cup grated Parmesan cheese

¼ cup butter, softened and cut into cubes

Instructions

Boil the potatoes in a large pot of salted water for 20–25 minutes or until fork-tender. Remove from the heat and drain.

In a large bowl, add the potatoes and all the remaining ingredients and mix with an electric mixer until combined. Add salt and pepper to taste.

Makes 4 servings

Corn Soufflé

My friend Lauren brought this to Thanksgiving dinner one year, and I found myself going back—for not only seconds, but for thirds. I had no idea how easy this was to make, and I can't say enough about how good it is.

Ingredients

1 (15-oz.) can corn niblets, with liquid

1 (15-oz.) creamed corn, with liquid

1 (8.5-oz.) box Jiffy corn muffin mix

1 cup sour cream

½ cup melted butter

Instructions

Preheat the oven to 350 degrees and lightly grease a 9-inch square baking dish.

In a medium bowl, mix all the ingredients together and bake for 50–60 minutes or until the soufflé is golden brown and the center is set.

Makes 8 servings

Feta and Tomato Asparagus

Feta is the perfect complement to the fresh tomato and asparagus in this side dish. Serve it with grilled chicken for a healthy dinner.

Ingredients

1 lb. asparagus, trimmed and chopped into 2-in. pieces

2 tsp. olive oil

salt to taste

2 tomatoes, seeded and diced

8 oz. crumbled feta cheese

Instructions

Preheat the oven to 400 degrees and line a baking sheet with foil.

Place the asparagus on the prepared sheet. Drizzle with the olive oil and sprinkle with salt.

Bake for 15–20 minutes or until tender.

Toss immediately with the tomatoes and feta and serve.

Makes 4 servings

Kimi's Sweet Potatoes

I despised sweet potatoes until my sister-in-law Kimi gave me this recipe. Let me tell you, this recipe has converted many sweet potato haters. With the brown sugar topping it could probably be classified as dessert, but I'm calling it a vegetable because I can.

Ingredients

Crust

1 cup brown sugar

⅓ cup flour

1 cup chopped pecans

⅓ cup butter, melted

Sweet Potato Mixture

3 cups cooked and mashed sweet potatoes (see note)

1 cup sugar

½ tsp. salt

1 tsp. vanilla

2 eggs, well beaten

½ cup butter, melted

Instructions

Preheat the oven to 375 degrees. Spray a medium-size casserole dish with nonstick spray.

For the crust: Combine the brown sugar, flour, pecans, and butter in a mixing bowl. Set aside.

Combine the sweet potatoes, sugar, salt, vanilla, eggs, and butter in a large mixing bowl in the order listed. Beat thoroughly with a hand mixer for about 3–4 minutes to increase the fluffiness of the sweet potato mixture. Add a splash of milk if needed, and mix.

Pour the mixture into the baking dish. Bake for 25 minutes. At this point, the dish can be covered and refrigerated for a couple of days if you are making it ahead of time.

Sprinkle the surface of the sweet potato mixture evenly with the crust mixture and return to the oven for 10 minutes. brown sugar and pecan crust should be slightly browned and crunchy. Allow to set at least 30 minutes before serving.

Makes 12 servings

To cook sweet potatoes: First, wash and dry them carefully. Next, you can either bake them at 400 degrees for 50–60 minutes, or boil them for 30 minutes, or 3. Pierce them with a fork and microwave them for 15–20 minutes.

Kaela's Blue Cheese Coleslaw

My friend Kaela might be the only person I know who comes close to loving food as much as I do. She's always entertaining and cooking for people. She has her own food blog at www.cookinandkickin.com. She gave me her family recipe for blue cheese coleslaw, which can stand alone as a side dish, or take a barbecue sandwich to a whole new level. We spend a lot of our holidays together, and I always know the food is going to be good.

Ingredients

1 (16-oz.) pkg. shredded coleslaw mix

¼ cup finely chopped sweet onion

½ cup apple cider vinegar

3 Tbsp. sugar

1 tsp. sea salt

½ cup mayonnaise

½ cup light sour cream

½ cup crumbled blue cheese, plus extra for garnish

salt and pepper

Instructions

In a large bowl, add the coleslaw and onion and toss together.

In a small saucepan, mix the vinegar, sugar, and salt. Stir together. Slowly bring the mixture to a simmer. Remove from the heat. The sugar should be dissolved.

Pour the warm vinegar mixture over the coleslaw mixture and toss. Let the coleslaw vinegar mixture sit for 15 minutes, tossing every 5 minutes to make sure it is coated evenly and is soaking up the juice evenly.

Put the coleslaw in a colander to drain for 5–10 minutes.

Put the drained coleslaw in a large bowl. Add the mayonnaise, sour cream, blue cheese, and a touch of salt and pepper.

Stir and mix until everything is evenly distributed.

Cover and chill for at least an hour before serving. Garnish with extra blue cheese before serving.

Makes 8 servings

Loaded Potato Slices

If you're craving a loaded baked potato but don't want to commit to a whole potato, try these loaded potato slices that have the same great flavor, but on a bite-sized scale.

Ingredients

2 Russet potatoes, unpeeled and washed

2 Tbsp. butter, melted

garlic salt

1 cup cheddar cheese

½ cup cooked, crumbled bacon

¼ cup chopped green onions

1 cup sour cream

Instructions

Preheat the oven to 400 degrees and line a baking sheet with foil.

Slice the potatoes into ¼-inch slices and brush both sides with butter. Lay on a baking sheet, sprinkle with the garlic salt, and bake for 20–30 minutes or until golden brown.

Remove from the oven and top with the cheese, bacon, and green onions. Return to the oven for 1–2 minutes or until the cheese is melted.

Remove from the oven. Serve with a dollop of sour cream.

Makes 16 servings

Creamed Corn

My mother-in-law gave me this recipe for creamed corn a couple years ago. I like it because, unlike most creamed corn recipes, it isn't swimming in cream, but it still has that creamy texture we all crave.

Ingredients

1 lb. frozen corn

1½ cups whipping cream

½ tsp. salt

2 Tbsp. sugar

pinch of pepper

1½ Tbsp. butter

1½ Tbsp. flour

3 Tbsp. grated Parmesan cheese

Instructions

Preheat the broiler and lightly grease a small baking dish.

Combine the corn, cream, salt, sugar, and pepper in a pot and bring to a boil. Simmer for 5 minutes.

Melt the butter in a small saucepan. Add the flour and cook for 1–2 minutes. Add the roux to the corn, mix well, and remove from the heat.

Transfer the corn mixture to the baking dish. Sprinkle with Parmesan cheese and brown under the broiler for a few minutes.

Makes 6 servings

desserts

S'mores Cups

My kids love to make s'mores, and to be honest it's an inherently sticky mess that I dread. Sometimes I want the s'more flavor without all that mess, and these s'mores cups are just the trick with their graham cracker crust, marshmallow center, and chocolate top.

Ingredients

½ cup butter, softened

¼ cup sugar

½ cup brown sugar

1 egg

1 tsp. vanilla extract

1¼ cups flour

1 cup graham cracker crumbs

1 tsp. baking powder

½ tsp. salt

½ cup chocolate chips

1 cup marshmallow fluff

2 (1.55-oz.) Hershey's chocolate bars

Instructions

Preheat the oven to 350 degrees. Spray a mini muffin tin with cooking spray. In a large bowl, cream the butter and sugars until light and fluffy, for about 2 minutes. Add the egg and vanilla and mix until combined.

In a separate bowl, whisk together the flour, graham cracker crumbs, baking powder, and salt. Add the flour mixture to the wet ingredients a little bit at a time until just incorporated. Gently stir chocolate chips into the dough.

Spoon marshmallow fluff into a resealable plastic bag and snip off the corner.

Press one rounded teaspoon of dough into each muffin tin. Pipe a teaspoon of marshmallow fluff on top of the dough in each muffin tin. Take a teaspoon of dough and flatten it in the palm of your hand and place it on top of the marshmallow fluff, repeating with the remaining cups.

Bake the cups for 7–9 minutes or until light golden brown.

Let the cups cool for 3–4 minutes in the muffin tins, then gently press one Hershey's chocolate square on top of each cup. Continue to let them cool in the pan. Remove and serve.

Makes 2 dozen cups

Cookie Crusted Chocolate Chip Cake

This cake has a crust made out of crispy chocolate chip cookie with an incredibly moist cake inside and mini chocolate chips throughout.

Ingredients

Cake

1 (16.5-oz.) pkg. refrigerated chocolate chip cookie dough

1 (15.25-oz.) yellow cake mix

1 (3.4-oz.) pkg. instant vanilla pudding mix

½ cup oil

4 eggs

1 cup sour cream

1 cup mini chocolate chips

Ganache

½ cup chocolate chips

3 Tbsp. butter

Make sure that you do not overbake this. Overbaking it can make it mediocre, but if baked correctly, the cookie crust with a moist cake inside is out of this world.

Instructions

Preheat the oven to 350 degrees. Thoroughly grease a Bundt pan.

Remove the cookie dough from the package and slice into ½-inch discs. Press the disks together in the bottom and side of the Bundt pan.

For the cake: In a mixing bowl, add the cake mix, vanilla pudding, oil, eggs, and sour cream. Mix until combined. Fold in the chocolate chips. Pour the batter on top of the pressed cookie dough in the Bundt pan.

Bake for 40–50 minutes or until the center is cooked. Cover with foil during baking if the top begins to brown too much.

Let the cake cool for 10 minutes, then invert onto a serving plate.

For the ganache: In a microwave safe bowl, heat the chocolate chips and butter for about 30 seconds or until the butter is melted. Stir together until smooth. Drizzle over the cooled cake. Serve with ice cream.

Makes 16 servings

Peanut Buster Delight

This dessert has an Oreo crust topped with a peanut butter pudding layer, whipped cream, and a sprinkle of peanut butter cups, peanuts, and syrup. It tastes incredibly light, yet sinful at the same time.

Ingredients

Crust

2 cups Oreo cookie crumbs

2 Tbsp. sugar

⅓ cup butter, melted

Filling

1 (5.1-oz.) instant vanilla pudding mix

3 cups milk

1 cup creamy peanut butter

Topping

2 cups heavy cream

¼ cup sugar

6 peanut butter cups, chopped

½ cup salted peanuts

2 Tbsp. chocolate syrup

Instructions

Preheat the oven to 350 degrees. Combine the Oreo crumbs, sugar, and butter in a medium bowl. Press into a 9 × 13 baking dish. Bake for 5–6 minutes; let cool.

In a separate bowl, add the pudding mix and milk and beat for 2–3 minutes. Transfer to the refrigerator to set. Once the pudding has set, fold in the peanut butter. Pour the pudding mixture onto the cooled crust.

For the topping: Beat the cream and sugar until stiff peaks form. Spread on top of the peanut butter layer. Top with the peanut butter cups, peanuts, and chocolate drizzle.

Makes 14 servings

Is it too hot to turn your oven on? You can turn this into a no-bake treat by chilling the crust instead of baking it. I've done it both ways, and I prefer the slight toasty flavor of baked crust, but it is good either way. If you want to take the peanut butter flavor even more over the top, microwave 2 tablespoons of peanut butter for about 10 seconds in a microwave safe bowl and drizzle it on top, in addition to the chocolate syrup.

Sugar Cookie Bars

I love traditional sugar cookies, but don't love all of the work that goes into them. These sugar cookie bars are an easy alternative—with no rolling required! I wanted to make a cookie bar with a soft and chewy texture, and I think I succeeded.

Ingredients

Cookies
1 cup butter, softened
1½ cups sugar
2 eggs
1½ tsp. vanilla or almond extract
3½ cups flour
½ tsp. baking soda
½ tsp. salt

Frosting
4 oz. cream cheese, softened
½ cup butter, softened
2½ cups powdered sugar
½ tsp. vanilla
2–3 Tbsp. milk
sprinkles for decoration

Instructions

Preheat the oven to 350 degrees and line a 9 × 13 baking dish with parchment paper or spray with cooking spray.

For the bars: In a large bowl, beat the butter and sugar until light and fluffy.

Add the eggs and extract and mix until combined.

In a separate bowl, whisk together the flour, baking soda, and salt.

Slowly add the flour mixture to the egg mixture and mix until combined.

Press the dough into the baking dish and bake for 18–20 minutes or until edges begin to have a touch of golden brown.

Remove from the oven and let the bars cool in the pan.

For the frosting: Beat the cream cheese and butter until fluffy. Add the powdered sugar and vanilla and beat until creamy. Add a tablespoon of milk at a time until the frosting reaches the consistency you desire.

Frost the cooled bars and top with sprinkles. Cut into bars and serve.

Makes 2 dozen bars

Darrell's Fudge

My friend's husband, Darrell, makes the best fudge in the world. While most recipes are extremely temperamental, this recipe is easy and extremely forgiving. You can even get creative with the flavors—use half peanut butter chips, all dark chocolate chips, or whatever you like.

Ingredients

3 cups sugar

1 cup evaporated milk

½ cup butter

1 cup milk chocolate chips

1 cup semi-sweet chocolate chips

1 (7-oz.) container marshmallow fluff

1 tsp. vanilla extract

Instructions

In a non-stick pot, bring the sugar, milk, and butter to a boil. Once it comes to a rolling boil, turn the stove down to medium heat and boil for exactly 5 minutes.

Remove from the heat and stir in the chocolate chips. Stir diligently until combined.

Add the marshmallow fluff. Stir until creamy. Add the vanilla and stir until combined.

Spoon into a foil-lined 9 × 13 pan and allow to cool completely. Cut into squares and serve.

Makes 16 servings

English Toffee Cookies

My sweet neighbor, Karen Wells, gave me this recipe at my bridal shower. She lived next door to me my entire life, and our families were close friends. Every Christmas, she would bring us a huge platter of tasty cookies. She recently passed away suddenly, and I now treasure this recipe with all my heart. These cookies taste just like toffee in cookie form, and they melt in your mouth instantly.

Ingredients

Cookies

1 cup butter

1 cup brown sugar

1 egg, beaten

1 tsp. vanilla extract

2 cups flour

Topping

1½ cups milk chocolate chips

¼ cup chopped almonds

Instructions

Preheat the oven to 350 degrees and line a cookie sheet with parchment paper.

Cream the butter and brown sugar in a medium bowl. Add the egg and vanilla and mix until combine. Add the flour and mix well. The dough will be very wet.

Drop by tablespoons onto the cookie sheet. Bake for 13–15 minutes or until golden brown. Remove from the oven and let cool.

In a small microwave-safe bowl, melt the chocolate chips. Spread over the cookies and top with chopped almonds.

Makes 2 dozen cookies

Strawberry Shortbread Pizza

I created this shortbread pizza because shortbread is one of my most favorite indulgences. The shortbread crust is smothered with a tangy cream cheese filling, and topped with fresh strawberries. You can use any kind of berry you like, but I prefer strawberries.

Ingredients

Crust

1 cup flour

¼ cup sugar

½ cup butter

½ cup chopped pecans

Filling

1 (8-oz.) pkg. cream cheese, softened

1 (14-oz.) can sweetened condensed milk

¼ cup lemon juice

1 tsp. vanilla extract

Topping

2 Tbsp. strawberry preserves

2 cups hulled and sliced strawberries

Instructions

Preheat the oven to 350 degrees.

For the crust: In a bowl, combine the flour and sugar. Cut in the butter until crumbly. Stir in the pecans. Press the mixture into an ungreased 12-inch pizza pan. Bake for 8–10 minutes or until the edges start to brown. Remove and let cool.

For the filling: In a medium bowl, beat the cream cheese, sweetened condensed milk, lemon juice, and vanilla until smooth. Spread the filling over the cooled crust.

For the topping: In a small bowl, microwave the strawberry preserves for 20–30 seconds or until runny. Let cool. Arrange the strawberries on top of the filling and drizzle with preserves.

Chill until ready to serve.

Makes 8 servings

Saltine Cracker Caramel Stacks

This is a simple no-bake treat that looks much harder than it actually is. Layers of saltine crackers and caramel are stacked in a pan, and topped with a layer of chocolate.

Ingredients

48 saltine crackers

1 (14-oz.) can sweetened condensed milk

¾ cup butter

½ cup brown sugar

3 Tbsp. light corn syrup

1 cup semi-sweet chocolate chips

Instructions

Line a 9-inch square baking pan with foil and spray it with cooking spray. Arrange 16 crackers in a single layer in the pan.

In a large saucepan, combine the sweetened condensed milk, butter, brown sugar, and corn syrup. Bring the mixture to a boil, stirring often. Reduce the heat and continue to cook at a low boil for 7 minutes. Remove from the heat and pour ⅓ of the mixture over the crackers. Repeat the cracker and caramel layers two more times.

Sprinkle the chocolate chips over the last layer of warm caramel and let them sit for about 3 minutes. Once chocolate chips are slightly melted, spread them evenly over the bars with a spatula.

Chill the pan for 2 hours or until the caramel has set.

Cut into bars and serve.

Makes 16 servings

Chewy Chocolate Peanut Butter Cookies

For some reason, something about Sunday always beckons me to make cookies. My rule for my kids is that if you don't help make the cookies, you don't get to lick the bowl. As you can imagine, I always have lots of helpers by my side. These are chewy chocolate cookies with little jewels of peanut butter throughout.

Ingredients

1¼ cups butter, softened

1 cup sugar

1 cup brown sugar

2 large eggs

2 tsp. vanilla extract

2¼ cups flour

¾ cup unsweetened cocoa

1 tsp. baking soda

½ tsp. salt

2 cups peanut butter chips

Instructions

Preheat the oven to 350 degrees and line a cookie sheet with parchment paper.

In a large bowl, cream the butter and sugars until light and fluffy.

Add the eggs and vanilla and mix until combined.

In a separate bowl, combine the flour, cocoa, baking soda and salt. Slowly add the flour mixture to the egg mixture and mix until combined. Stir in the peanut butter chips.

Drop the dough by tablespoons onto the cookie sheet. Bake for 8–9 minutes. Do not overbake! Let the cookies rest on the cookie sheet for a few minutes before moving to the cooling rack.

Makes 2 dozen cookies

Chewy Blondies

As much as I love chocolate, every once in a while I crave a non-chocolate dessert. What I love about these blondies is their chewy balance of sweet and salty. I use all brown sugar to keep them as soft and chewy as possible.

Ingredients

1 cup butter, melted

2 cups brown sugar

2 eggs

2 tsp. vanilla extract

2 cups flour

¼ tsp. salt

1 cup chopped pecans

1 cup white chocolate chips

Instructions

Preheat the oven to 375 degrees and line a 9 × 13 baking pan with aluminum foil, allowing excess foil to hang over the sides.

In a large bowl, cream the butter and sugar together. Beat in the eggs and vanilla. Stir in the flour and salt. Add the pecans and white chocolate chips and stir until combined.

Spread evenly in the pan and bake for 30–35 minutes or until top is golden brown. Let the bars cool in the pan. Lift the bars out of the pan using the aluminum foil and cut into squares.

Makes 12 servings

Oreo Truffles

My sister-in-law Kristy introduced these to me when she joined our family. I have to say, if I could pick one dessert to eat the rest of my life, this would be it. Mind you, this is coming from someone who has eaten her fair share of desserts. Kristy has her own food blog at www.sweettreatsmore.com.

Ingredients

36 Oreo cookies

1 (8-oz.) pkg. cream cheese, softened

16 oz. melting chocolate, melted

Instructions

Crush the cookies finely in a food processor. In a medium bowl, add the cream cheese and mix until thoroughly combined.

Roll into 1-inch balls and place on a baking sheet or tray. Freeze until firm, about 30–60 minutes. Do not skip this step!

Using a fork, dip the Oreo balls into melted chocolate coating, tapping the fork on the side to get excess off, and place on wax paper until hardened.

Refrigerate until ready to serve.

Makes 8 servings

 If you don't have a food processor, you can crush your Oreos in a resealable plastic bag.

Nutella Cheesecake Stuffed Strawberries

My favorite way to eat Nutella is with a spoon. Second to that is in these cheesecake stuffed strawberries. It's almost like eating an inside-out chocolate dipped strawberry.

Ingredients

1 (8-oz.) package cream cheese, softened

½ cup Nutella

⅓ cup powdered sugar

1 pound strawberries, hulled

Instructions

In a medium bowl, mix together the cream cheese, Nutella, and powdered sugar.

Place the mixture in a large, resealable plastic bag. Cut off the corner with a pair of scissors. Fill each strawberry with about 1 tablespoon of the mixture.

Refrigerate until ready to serve.

Makes 16 servings

Cinnamon Roll Sheet Cake

I love the melt-in-your-mouth texture of sheet cakes, and thought a cinnamon roll version would be out of this world. I was right! Like most sheet cakes, this cake is even better the second day because it's even more moist, and the flavors have blended together.

Ingredients

Cake
1 cup butter, softened

1 cup water

2 cups flour

2 cups sugar

2 eggs, beaten

½ cup sour cream

1 tsp. vanilla extract

1 tsp. baking soda

1 tsp. salt

Filling
1 cup brown sugar

½ cup butter, melted

1½ Tbsp. ground cinnamon

1 Tbsp. flour

Frosting
4 oz. cream cheese, softened

4 Tbsp. butter, softened

2 cups powdered sugar

½ tsp. vanilla extract

Instructions

Preheat the oven to 375 degrees and grease a 10 × 15 × 1 baking pan.

For the cake: In a medium saucepan, bring the butter and water to a boil. While the mixture is boiling, add the flour and sugar to a large bowl and mix. Add the eggs, sour cream, vanilla, baking soda, and salt and mix until combined.

Pour in the boiling butter/water mixture, a little at a time until completely combined, stirring constantly. The batter will be very thin. Pour the batter into the prepared pan.

For the filling: In a small bowl, combine the brown sugar, butter, cinnamon, and flour. Place dollops of the mixture on top of the cake batter, making sure to evenly distribute it. Swirl gently with a knife, making sure not to mix.

Bake for 18–22 minutes or until golden brown. Remove from oven and cool for 5–10 minutes before frosting.

For the frosting: In a medium bowl, beat the cream cheese and butter until fluffy. Add the powdered sugar and vanilla and beat for 2–3 minutes. Spread the frosting on the cake. Cut into squares and serve.

Makes 24 servings

Buckeye Dip

This dip tastes just like a light version of your favorite Buckeye candy. It's loaded with peanut butter flavor and dotted with chocolate chips. You can add the ganache on top to dress it up a bit, but it's also good without it. I usually like to use fresh whipped cream in everything, but for this dip I've found that the whipped topping stabilizes the dip, whereas fresh whipped cream deflates after a while. I literally had to hide this from myself, which is unfortunately an easier task these days than it should be.

Ingredients

4 oz. cream cheese, softened

½ cup creamy peanut butter

1 cup powdered sugar

2 Tbsp. milk

8 oz. frozen whipped topping, thawed

1 cup mini chocolate chips

graham crackers

Ganache

¼ cup milk chocolate chips

2 Tbsp. butter

Instructions

In a medium bowl, add the cream cheese and peanut butter and beat until creamy. Add the powdered sugar and milk and mix until combined.

Fold in the whipped topping until well combined. Fold in the chocolate chips.

For the ganache: Melt the butter and chocolate chips in the microwave and stir until creamy. Drizzle on top of the dip and place in the refrigerator to set up.

Serve with graham crackers or apple slices.

Makes 10 servings

Dutch Apple Pie

I'm very open about the fact that I'm terrible at making pie crusts. But for this pie, there are no crusts to mess up—the crumble on top doubles as the crust in the pie. I like a lot of crumble on my pie, and whoa mama, this pie has plenty.

Ingredients

Crumble

2½ cups flour

1¼ cups brown sugar

¾ cup quick oats

1 cup butter, melted

Filling

½ cup sugar

3 Tbsp. cornstarch

1 cup water

3 cups diced and peeled apples

1 tsp. vanilla extract

½ tsp. cinnamon

2 tsp. lemon juice

Instructions

Preheat the oven to 375 degrees.

In a large bowl, combine the flour, brown sugar, oats, and butter. Reserve 1½ cups for the top of the pie and press the remaining mixture on the bottom and sides of a 9-inch pie pan.

For the filling: In a saucepan, combine the sugar, cornstarch, and water. Bring the mixture to a boil until it becomes nice and thick. Remove from the heat and stir in the apples, vanilla, cinnamon, and lemon juice. Pour the filling into the pie crust and top with reserved 1½ cups topping.

Bake for 35–45 minutes. If the pie begins to get too brown, cover with aluminum foil. Cool on a wire rack and serve with ice cream.

Makes 8 servings

Banana Split Brownie Pizza

If you love banana splits, you'll love this pizza. The pizza has a brownie crust, smothered with a pineapple cream cheese layer, and topped with your classic banana split toppings. I've been making this pizza for years and it's always a crowd pleaser.

Ingredients

1 (18.9-oz.) box brownie mix

1 (8-oz.) pkg. cream cheese, softened

1 (8-oz.) can crushed pineapple, drained

2 Tbsp. sugar

1 banana, sliced and tossed in lemon juice to keep from browning

1 cup sliced strawberries

½ cup chopped nuts

chocolate syrup

Instructions

Preheat the oven to 350 degrees and spray a 15-inch pizza pan with cooking spray. Make sure you use a pan with an edge so your batter doesn't spill. Prepare the brownie mix according to the package directions and pour into the pizza pan. Bake for 18–20 minutes, or until the center is cooked.

In a small bowl, combine the cream cheese, pineapple, and sugar. Mix well. Spread the mixture over the cooled brownie.

Arrange the fruit on top of the pizza. Sprinkle with nuts. Drizzle with chocolate syrup right before serving. Cut into slices and serve.

Makes 8 servings

Janessa's Chex Mix

My friend Janessa brought this over as a treat once, and I think I ate it all myself. I love that she chops the coconut finely, so that even those who don't like the texture of coconut can barely detect it in there.

Ingredients

1¾ cups coconut

1 cup sugar

1 cup light corn syrup

pinch of salt

1½ cups butter

1 tsp. vanilla extract

½ tsp. baking soda

1¼ cups sliced almonds

6 cups corn or rice Chex cereal

Instructions

Chop the coconut in a food processor. Add the coconut, cereal, and almonds to a large bowl. Combine the sugar, corn syrup, salt, and butter in a large microwave-safe bowl. Microwave for 5 minutes. Stir and cook for 2 more minutes.

Add the vanilla and baking soda, then pour the mixture over the dry ingredients. Stir thoroughly to combine.

Makes 30 servings

German Chocolate Brownies

I've had many versions of these, but this version from my friend BriAnne is by far the best. These are soft brownies with a sweet caramel layer in the middle.

Ingredients

½ cup butter

⅔ cup evaporated milk, divided

1 (15.25-oz.) box German chocolate cake mix

1 (14-oz.) bag Kraft caramels (about 50 caramels)

2 cups milk chocolate chips

Instructions

Preheat the oven to 350 degrees.

Melt the butter and mix together with ⅓ cup of the evaporated milk and the cake mix. Press half of the mixture into an ungreased 9 × 13 baking pan. It will be a thin layer. Bake for 6 minutes.

Place the remaining ⅓ cup evaporated milk and the caramels in a microwave-safe bowl. Microwave for 3 minutes, stirring after each minute.

Pour 1 cup of chocolate chips over the baked brownies, straight out of the oven. Pour caramel sauce over the chocolate chips. Top with the crumbled pieces of the remaining brownie mixture and chocolate chips.

Bake for 15 minutes. Cool completely and cut into squares.

Makes 24 servings

Oatmeal Cranberry Cookies

These cookies have a hearty texture that almost makes me think they're healthy. Wishful thinking, I know, but I love this flavor combination of oats, dried cranberries, white chocolate chips, and nuts. You can replace half of the flour with whole wheat flour to make them a little healthier. Cornstarch is the secret ingredient that keeps these cookies thick and soft.

Ingredients

1 cup butter, softened

1 cup brown sugar

1 egg

1 egg yolk

1 tsp. vanilla extract

2 cups flour

1½ tsp. baking soda

2 tsp. cornstarch

½ tsp. salt

2 cups old-fashioned rolled oats

1 cup dried cranberries

1 cup white chocolate chips

½ cup chopped walnuts

Instructions

Preheat the oven to 350 degrees and line a cookie sheet with parchment paper.

In a large bowl, beat together the butter and brown sugar until fluffy. Add the eggs and vanilla and mix until combined.

In a separate bowl, stir the flour, baking soda, cornstarch, and salt together. Slowly add the flour mixture to the butter mixture and mix until incorporated. Add the oats, cranberries, white chocolate chips, and nuts and mix until combined.

Roll into balls, about 1½ tablespoons in size, and place onto the prepared sheet. Flatten slightly with your hand.

Bake for 8–10 minutes or until the edges are golden brown. Let the cookies cool for a couple of minutes on the pan. Move them to a wire rack to cool completely.

Makes 6 dozen cookies

Key Lime Pie

My husband and I are always actively searching for the best key lime pie out there. We order it at every restaurant we dine at. I've found that I prefer key lime pies without egg yolks in the filling, which give it a flan texture. This version is lighter in color and texture. I'm lucky to live in Florida where key limes are readily accessible, but if you don't have access to key limes, use regular limes instead. The result is a little less tart, but it will still have a bright lime taste.

Ingredients

Crust

1¼ cups graham cracker crumbs

3 Tbsp. sugar

⅓ cup butter, melted

Filling

2 (14-oz.) cans sweetened
   condensed milk

½ cup sour cream

¾ cup Key lime juice

2 tsp. grated lime zest, plus
   extra for topping

whipped cream

Instructions

Preheat the oven 350 degrees.

For the crust: In a medium bowl, combine the graham cracker crumbs, sugar, and butter. Press the mixture firmly into the bottom and sides of a 9-inch pie plate. Bake for 8 minutes. Remove from the oven and let the crust cool while preparing the filling.

In a medium bowl, add the sweetened condensed milk, sour cream, Key lime juice, and lime zest. Mix until combined and pour into the graham cracker crust.

Bake for 7–8 minutes or until little bubbles appear on the surface of the pie. Remove from the oven and chill for 2–3 hours before serving. Serve with whipped cream and garnish with lime zest.

Makes 12 servings

Double Cake Batter Cookies

These cake batter cookies, drizzled with cake batter frosting, have to be one of the most decadent treats I've ever had. If you're like me, you'll find all kinds of things to smother with this cake batter frosting—brownies, graham crackers, cookies, you name it.

Ingredients

Cookies

1 (15.25-oz.) yellow cake mix

2 eggs

⅔ cup oil

¼ cup sprinkles, plus extra for topping

Cake Batter Frosting

6 Tbsp. butter, softened

3½ cups powdered sugar

1 tsp. vanilla extract

¾ cup cake mix

4–6 Tbsp. milk

Instructions

Preheat the oven to 350 degrees. Line a cookie sheet with parchment paper or lightly spray with cooking spray.

In a large bowl combine the cake mix, eggs, and oil and blend well. Fold in the sprinkles.

Drop by tablespoons onto the cookie sheet and bake for 8–10 minutes. Do not overbake. The cookies will still be pale in color. Remove from the oven and let them cool on the cookie sheet.

For the Cake Batter Frosting: In a medium bowl, combine the butter, powdered sugar, vanilla, cake mix, and 4 tablespoons of the milk. Beat until fluffy, adding 1–2 more tablespoons of milk to reach desired consistency.

Frost cooled cookies and top with sprinkles.

Makes 2 dozen cookies

*I like to fill a **resealable plastic bag** with the frosting and cut off the corner for easy piping.*

Oatmeal Raisin Cookie Dough Dip

If you're a cookie dough snitcher like me, you'll appreciate this dip. Oatmeal raisin cookie dough is one thing I would actually rather eat in dough form than as a cookie.

Ingredients

1 (8-oz.) pkg. cream cheese, softened

½ cup butter, slightly softened

2 cups powdered sugar

4 Tbsp. brown sugar

1 tsp. vanilla extract

½ cup flour

2 tsp. cinnamon

2½ cups quick oats

¾ cup raisins

milk (optional)

Instructions

In a large bowl, beat the cream cheese, butter, powdered sugar, brown sugar, and vanilla until creamy.

Add the flour and cinnamon and mix until combined.

Stir in the oats and raisins. Add milk if you want a thinner consistency.

Serve with vanilla wafers, graham crackers, or apples for dipping.

Makes 8 servings

Cooking Measurement Equivalents

Cups	Tablespoons	Fluid Ounces
⅛ cup	2 Tbsp.	1 fl. oz.
¼ cup	4 Tbsp.	2 fl. oz.
⅓ cup	5 Tbsp. + 1 tsp.	
½ cup	8 Tbsp.	4 fl. oz.
⅔ cup	10 Tbsp. + 2 tsp.	
¾ cup	12 Tbsp.	6 fl. oz.
1 cup	16 Tbsp.	8 fl. oz.

Cups	Fluid Ounces	Pints/Quarts/Gallons
1 cup	8 fl. oz.	½ pint
2 cups	16 fl. oz.	1 pint = ½ quart
3 cups	24 fl. oz.	1½ pints
4 cups	32 fl. oz.	2 pints = 1 quart
8 cups	64 fl. oz.	2 quarts = ½ gallon
16 cups	128 fl. oz.	4 quarts = 1 gallon

Other Helpful Equivalents

1 Tbsp.	3 tsp.
8 oz.	½ lb.
16 oz.	1 lb.

Metric Measurement Equivalents

Approximate Weight Equivalents

Ounces	Pounds	Grams
4 oz.	¼ lb.	113 g
5 oz.		142 g
6 oz.		170 g
8 oz.	½ lb.	227 g
9 oz.		255 g
12 oz.	¾ lb.	340 g
16 oz.	1 lb.	454 g

Approximate Volume Equivalents

Cups	US Fluid Ounces	Milliliters
⅛ cup	1 fl. oz.	30 ml
¼ cup	2 fl. oz.	59 ml
½ cup	4 fl. oz.	118 ml
¾ cup	6 fl. oz.	177 ml
1 cup	8 fl. oz.	237 ml

Other Helpful Equivalents

½ tsp.	2½ ml	
1 tsp.	5 ml	
1 Tbsp.	15 ml	

Index

About the Author

Christy is a self-proclaimed foodaholic. She grew up in Mesa, Arizona, as the youngest of ten kids, and has forty nieces and nephews and counting. Food and family were always intertwined in her childhood, and most of her memories revolve around food. She took ballet and contemporary dance for fourteen years and played the viola for ten years. Music is a big part of her life, which is why on any given day you can hear her in the kitchen with the tunes cranking! She graduated from Brigham Young University in computer science, and worked at a forensic science software company until 2005, when she had her first son.

Christy always loved food, but she didn't really start cooking and baking until she got married and realized she needed to feed that huge man of hers. She loves running and, ironically, most of her recipe ideas she comes up with during her runs. She started her blog *The Girl Who Ate Everything* in 2008 and worked as a freelance writer and recipe developer for General Mills starting in 2010. She's been married for thirteen years and has been living in sunny Florida for nine years, where her husband plays football for the Miami Dolphins. She is the mother of five kids and loves her life.